Jordan Lee Harding

Azerbaijan

Azerbaijan

Edited by
Tamara Dragadze

MELISENDE
London

© Fox Communications and Publications

All rights reserved. No part of this publication may be reproduced,
stored in a retrieval system, or transmitted in any form or
by any means, electronic, mechanical, photocopying, recording
or otherwise, without the prior permission of the copyright owner.

First published 2000 by
Melisende
An imprint of Fox Communications and Publications
39 Chelmsford Road
London E18 2PW
England
tel: +44 (0)20 8 498 9768
fax: +44 (0)20 8 504 2558
e-mail: M106040@cs.com

ISBN 1 901764 20 6

Editor: Leonard Harrow
Assistant editor: Alan Ball
Designer: Zena Flax

Printed and bound in Singapore

Contents

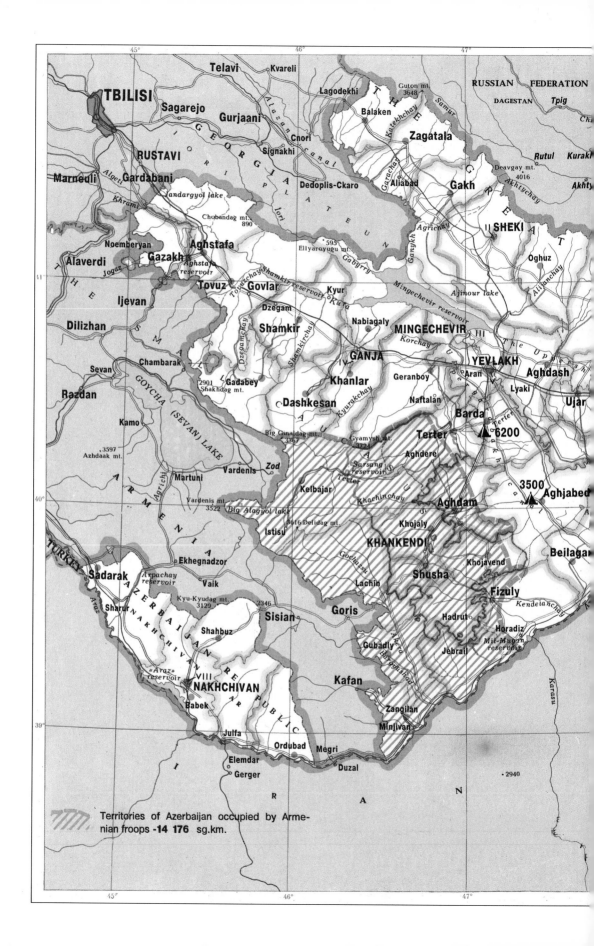

Territories of Azerbaijan occupied by Armenian froops -14 176 sg.km.

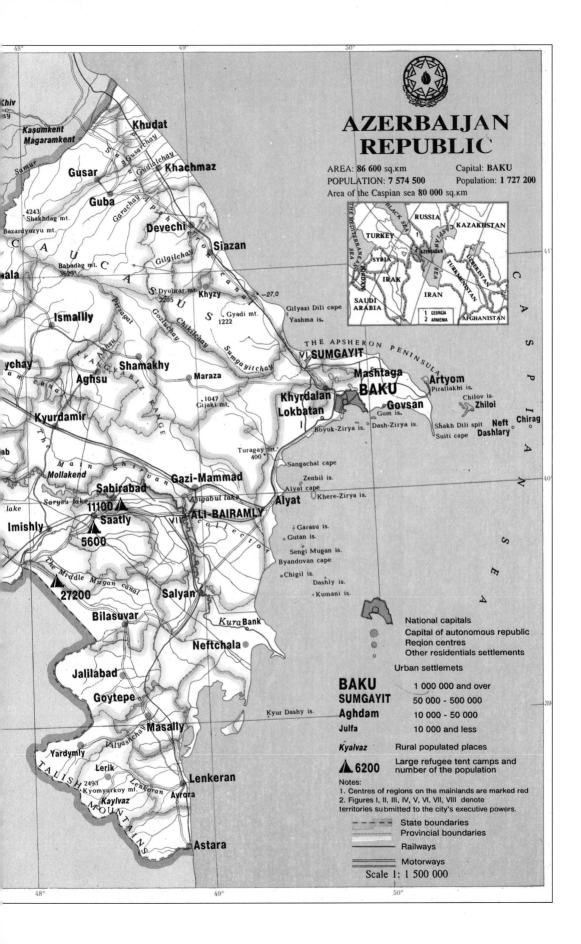

AZERBAIJAN REPUBLIC

AREA: **86 600** sq.км   Capital: **BAKU**
POPULATION: **7 574 500**   Population: **1 727 200**
Area of the Caspian sea **80 000** sq.км

National capitals	
Capital of autonomous republic	
Region centres	
Other residentials settlements	

Urban settlemets

BAKU — 1 000 000 and over
SUMGAYIT — 50 000 - 500 000
Aghdam — 10 000 - 50 000
Julfa — 10 000 and less

Kyalvaz — Rural populated places

▲ **6200** — Large refugee tent camps and number of the population

Notes:
1. Centres of regions on the mainlands are marked red
2. Figures I, II, III, IV, V, VI, VII, VIII denote territories submitted to the city's executive powers.

- - - - — State boundaries
       — Provincial boundaries
───── — Railways
═════ — Motorways

Scale 1: 1 500 000

9

Steve Remp, Chief Executive of Ramco, and Natiq Aliyev,
President of the State Oil Company of the Azerbaijan Republic
(seated second left and left), sign a Production Sharing
Agreement for Ramco's onshore Muradkhanli field, in the
presence of British Prime Minister Rt Hon Tony Blair and the
President of Azerbaijan, Heydar Aliyev, on 21 July 1998 during
President Aliyev's official visit to the UK.

Preface from Ramco Energy plc

Ramco Energy plc is delighted to have been able to contribute to this defining publication on Azerbaijan, its politics, its history, its people and its culture. There has long been a need for a concise account of this great country, and we hope that this will fill a gap as well as being of great interest to a number of audiences.

Ramco is a leading oil exploration and production company, and has a long history of involvement in Azerbaijan since I made my first visit in 1989 and became the first Western oilman to enter the country since the 1920s. As a founding partner in the Azerbaijan International Operating Company, Ramco secured a carried interest in the development of the super-giant Azeri, Chirag and Deep Water Gunashli fields and in 1998 signed a Production Sharing Contract with the State Oil Company of Azerbaijan covering the onshore Muradkhanli field, believed to be Azerbaijan's largest. The Company is also in negotiations with SOCAR on further projects within Azerbaijan.

We trust that this publication will promote international understanding of the Republic of Azerbaijan, and the myriad of opportunities that this great country has to offer.

Steve Remp *Chairman and Chief Executive*

Baku, School for
gifted children

Editor's Preface

This book has been compiled entirely from texts supplied by staff of the Azerbaijan Academy of Sciences, the President's Administration of the Azerbaijan Republic and the Economic Section of the Azerbaijan Embassy in London. The editor would like to thank the Embassy staff, particularly Heydar Efendiev and Altai Efendiev. Likewise thanks go to Jane Weale for her help with the geographical section and Nick Ryan at Policy Partnership for assistance with the administrative aspects of producing the work. The editor would also like to thank Sir Malcolm Rifkind at Ramco for his support.

Wherever possible, the Azerbaijani version of names and their spelling have been used.

Tamara Dragadze, BA (Kent), DPhil (Oxon)
Editor

Introduction

Azerbaijan is a land of contrasts, from its varied geographical features to its cultural mix of East and West. It has a rich and ancient history, yet it has also embraced the perquisites of modern life with enthusiasm. Baku boasts a medieval quarter with an old tower and several restored hostelries that used to serve the caravanserai of the Silk Road. Elsewhere in the country – in cities such as Ganja, for instance – efforts are being made to restore historic buildings. Baku also contains shining new office buildings which house the growing infrastructure of a modernising economy; mosques and churches of a variety of denominations; and embassies and foreign institutions demonstrating the reintegration of Azerbaijan into the international arena. The roofs of houses in Baku, the capital, bristle with satellite dishes and television aerials. There are, in addition, endeavours to bring about changes in rural activities necessary for a developing economy linked to the global market.

All these contrasts, however, are confusing to the newcomer. Learning a little about the historical background of Azerbaijan and becoming acquainted with some of the physical features and natural resources of the country can go a long way in helping one to appreciate this fascinating country.

HISTORICAL BACKGROUND

Azerbaijan has a rich and ancient history. On its territory, a treasury of world culture was created over several thousand years, so one can trace the development of human civilisation through many stages.

**Mingechaur,
clay pot from 4th–3rd
centuries BC**

Gobustan

Evidence that early human life existed here can be found in the Stone Age site of the Azykh Cave. The Mannaean kingdom, considered to be one of the forerunners of statehood in Azerbaijan, developed in the ninth century BC. Deities, arranged in pantheons, were sculpted and worshipped, testifying to an advanced form of culture. It is also interesting to see the relics expressing Mannaean belief in the power of the sun and moon. The Medes conquered the Mannaean kingdom at the beginning of the sixth century BC. The official religion then became Zoroastrianism, in which fire was an important symbol, undoubtedly linked to the presence of oil and gas on the local territory which could be combusted spontaneously. It is presumed that the region became a place of pilgrimage for Zoroastrian devotees from far and near.

There is evidence to support the argument that statehood was established on the territory of Azerbaijan in ancient times. For example, it was here that there came into being, around the time of Alexander the Great, the satrapy of Atropatenes. It is often said that 'Azerbaijan' means 'the land of fire'. There is, however, a popular argument that 'Azerbaijan' is also a corrupted form of the name 'Atropatenes'.

Later the Albanian kingdom was established, no longer within the purview of Persia but as a sovereign state (known as 'Caucasian Albania', not to be confused with the Albania of the Balkans). The idea of statehood in Azerbaijan was strengthened in the third to fifth centuries AD when Christianity penetrated the territory. It was here that one of the first apostolic, autocephalous churches in the Southern Caucasus was established which further stimulated the growth of local culture. The appearance of the Albanian alphabet in the beginning of the fifth century was important for the development of educational institutions, of literature, and architectural traditions, remnants of which can still be seen in the present day.

By the beginning of the eighth century, Azerbaijan had been conquered by the Arabs, and it was then included in an Islamic caliphate and known as the province of Arran. From then on, over the centuries, Islam slowly became the predominant religion in Azerbaijan. Out of this, new traditions arose which were labelled 'Islamic', and a new cultural idiom was given to local scientists, poets and architects.

During the Middle Ages the various states which arose, either as part of larger entities or confined within the boundaries of the territory, were all distinguished in their form of administration and for promoting the arts. Shirvan was legendary, with Shemakha as its capital. The personality of one of its rulers, the Shirvanshah, was admired by de la Valle, an Italian traveller in the late medieval period, who wrote of the excellence of the Shirvanshah's wines and the flourishing of the arts at his court. It is unfortunate that an earthquake in the early twentieth century destroyed Shemakha but it was evoked longingly in many literary works emanating from the region. Likewise, the Sefevid state, with its early power base in the territory of Azerbaijan, possessed an able administration referred to repeatedly in the chronicles of the time.

The rivalry between neighbouring states, which attempted to bring the territory of Azerbaijan into their sphere of influence, had by the eighteenth century disrupted the relative stability of the previous centuries. Whereas in the twelfth century the state entities in Azerbaijan had survived the invasion of Seljuk Turks, now it was Russia, Ottoman Turkey and Persia who fought for the spoils of conquest. The result was a number of khanates – semi-independent state formations – spread over the territory with little internal unity.

above: A caravanserai
in Old Baku

right: Fragments of
glazed pottery, 12th–
13th centuries, found
underwater

Absheron, fortress

The most relevant event for modern Azerbaijan occurred at the beginning of the nineteenth century. The Treaty of Turkmenchay in 1828 between Russia and Persia finally divided Azerbaijan and its people: the northern half was annexed by Russia and became an integral part of the Tsarist Russian empire; the southern territory became a part of the Iranian state. Tabriz was the main city there and to this day it continues to be a focus of Azerbaijani identity within Iran. It is the northern half which forms the territory of the present day Azerbaijan Republic.

By the end of the nineteenth century, fundamental changes had occurred in Azerbaijan. Baku became known as a world centre for the extraction and processing of oil. At the turn of the century more than half of the entire world's, and ninety five per cent of Russian, oil was extracted there. The whole region was transformed, as an international business community developed and thrived. The Nobels made a fortune in Azerbaijan as did the Rothschilds. British engineers built the famous pipeline from Baku to Batumi on the Georgian coast. People of all nationalities − Azerbaijanis, Armenians, Georgians, North Caucasians and Russians as well as British, French, Germans, Scandinavians and others − built sumptuous houses, churches, clubs and restaurants. Above all, however, it was local culture which was transformed, in the cities especially. Newspapers and journals flourished, literature was prolific and the arts developed remarkably. Thus, the composer Uzeir Hajibeyov wrote the first classical opera in the Muslim world, *Leyli ve Mejnun*, which was premiered in 1908 in Baku. The city was proud of its opera house and its theatres at the time.

Azerbaijanis participated fully in these creative activities and the wealthier families became absorbed into mainstream European life, sending their young people to study in Berlin and elsewhere. One oil industry businessman in particular, Taghiyev, distinguished himself greatly through his generous support of journals and the arts; he personally sponsored many young people to study in foreign countries and he even opened a secondary school for girls. This ensured that at least the upper stratum of Azerbaijani society could lead the way to modernisation, high culture and an international perspective. It is this period of history in particular that present day Azerbaijanis hanker after, when Baku was a hub of cultural and business activity with representatives from the four corners of the earth.

During that period also, very lively political debate took place among Azerbaijanis, assisting the development of national self-consciousness and the desire for independence and sovereignty. Political parties of every conceivable hue were created and their ideas were discussed in a multitude of publications.

The fall of the Russian monarchy in February 1917 created favourable conditions for the further development of national movements in the periphery of the empire. On 28 May 1918, the independent Azerbaijan Democratic Republic was proclaimed. In its short life it accomplished some remarkable feats. For example, in 1918 new legislation established universal suffrage, giving women the vote before most European countries. It was also first among Muslim states to adopt the Latin alphabet instead of the Arabic script. It undertook land reform, was committed to founding institutions of higher education and established open government with a multi-party parliament. The national flag and anthem were adopted and, like the other republics of the South Caucasus, Azerbaijan was recognised by the League of Nations. Unfortunately, on 28 April 1920, the 11th Red Army invaded Baku and Azerbaijan soon became part of the USSR.

Baku, panorama

Azerbaijan experienced mixed fortunes as a Union Republic. Its oil wealth was expropriated by the central authority, with the result that it never possessed the economic advantage it should have had in the Soviet Union. On the other hand, some industries were developed, such as the manufacturing of air-conditioners and petroleum derivatives. The Azerbaijan Institute of Oil and Chemistry Studies was an outstanding achievement of the Soviet education system. When Siberian oil fields were discovered it was mostly Azerbaijan oil specialists who developed them, a further example of Azerbaijan's invaluable contributions to the Soviet Union as a whole. It shared in the same tragedies as the rest of the country but also benefited from some of the more enlightened policies. Universal education eradicated illiteracy and a rudimentary but universal health system was developed that reached the furthest corners of Azerbaijan. Likewise music, the arts and literature continued to thrive. Although Western commerce disappeared, Baku continued to be a multi-ethnic city and good relations existed with all Azerbaijan's neighbours.

It was only towards the end of the Soviet period that tensions became visible which were tolerated by the authorities, possibly with the aim of weakening the links between the peoples of the South Caucasus. When Azerbaijan began to reclaim its independence from Moscow it was punished unmercifully when Soviet tanks rampaged through Baku, killing bystanders indiscriminately. That event has been named 'Black January' and some of its victims are buried in the Martyrs' Alley near the Parliament.

On 18 October 1990, Azerbaijan declared independence. The Soviet Union came to a close by the end of that year. This allowed the country to control its own natural resources and to run its own affairs which, given its previous experience, was very important to

Martyrs' Alley

its citizens. The euphoria of independence, however, was marred by the continuing war with Armenia over Mountainous Garabagh, an autonomous region within Azerbaijan, continuing the conflict which had begun in 1988. A succession of presidents and governments was unable to stop the fighting and it inhibited the rapid reforms and development which the country had hoped for. In May 1994, Armenia and Azerbaijan, through direct contact, reached agreement on a ceasefire. Azerbaijan has lost control of twenty per cent of its territory but it is committed to a political solution to the dispute and does not see any advantage in a return to violence.

On 12 November 1995, the Constitution of the independent Azerbaijan Republic was adopted and received nationwide support in a national referendum. The census of 1999 showed that the population of Azerbaijan stands at around 8 million. There is an Azerbaijani majority but there are also representatives of many other nationalities, all of whom have the constitutional right to education, media and cultural activities in their own language. These include Russians, Talysh, Lesghins, Kurds, Mountain Jews, Georgians, Armenians, Khinalyg and Udines, each with their unique traditions and histories.

Baku, President's
Administration
Building

The Country in the Political Arena

At the close of the twentieth century Azerbaijan is a member of 31 international and regional organisations, including the United Nations (recognised March 1992); the Organisation for Security and Co-operation in Europe (accession in January 1992); NATO's Partnership for Peace Programme (March 1992); the Organisation of the Islamic Conference (joined 1992); the Commonwealth of Independent States (September 1993); the Council of Europe (special guest status, June 1996); the European Union Treaty on Partnership and Co-operation (1992); the Organization of Black Sea Economic Co-operation (1992); the European Bank for Reconstruction and Development (1992); the World Bank (1992); UNESCO (1992); UNICEF (1992); the World Health Organization (1992); the International Federation of the Red Cross and the Red Crescent; Interpol; the International Olympic Committee and others.

Azerbaijan's foreign policy is based on the protection and strengthening of national independence, territorial integrity, and the development of equal, co-operative and mutually profitable relations with all states of the world. It gives priority to its immediate neighbours and its traditional European trading partners, as well as promoting friendship with countries of the Islamic and Turkic world with whom some aspects of a common identity are recognised.

The main diplomatic efforts of Azerbaijan are directed towards finding a settlement of the Armenia-Azerbaijan conflict. Four resolutions were adopted by the UN Security Council (Nos 822, 853, 874, 884) for the restitution of occupied Azerbaijani territory and the return of refugees and displaced persons, but they have yet to be implemented. Neither has the release of Azerbaijani women hostages yet taken place in respect of the UN resolution following the 39th Session of the Commission on Women.

Azerbaijan participates actively in international summits and in the work of regional and sub-regional meetings and exhibitions. It is a signatory to a number of international treaties and agreements, most importantly the Convention on Human Rights, the Convention on Children's Rights and the Convention on the Elimination of Discrimination Against Women. Azerbaijan has also developed a network of commercial and political partners throughout the world which has been strengthened by the signatories to the oil contracts in which they participate.

Literature, Art and Music

Azerbaijan's geographical position and history have bequeathed the country a complex and varied cultural legacy.

The Azerbaijani school of literature was represented by some of the leading lights of the medieval world. First and foremost was the poet Nizami Ganjevi (of Ganja), famous especially for his work *Khamsa*. Others include Afsalladin Khagani, the female poet Mehseti Genjevi (also of the city of Ganja), Molla Penah Vagif and, of course, Fizuli. Khurshudbanu Natavan, another female poet, is also well known among scholars of the region. Later writers include Mirza Fatali Akhundov, the satirist Sabir and Jalil Memmedguluzade, whose works have been translated in part into other languages. During the Soviet period, some writers retained their integrity under difficult conditions and today younger writers are struggling to find a new identity in a different world.

In art also, Azerbaijan has drawn on its traditional background. Carpet weaving is an old and sophisticated art; so, too, are appliquè, enamel and metalwork. Architectural monuments are worth exploring, some dating back to the Nakhchivan and Shirvan schools, such as the Momina Khatun Tomb, the Maiden's Tower (Gyz Galasy) and the remains of the Shirvanshah's palace. Miniature paintings by Behruz Kengerli and the paintings of Settar Behlulzade and Tahir Salakhov have received worldwide acclaim. Today, young painters are also trying to find their place with their particular character in the world of modern art.

Music has always played an important part locally and it acquired

a more formal role with the development of a specific classical genre. In the thirteenth century, an outstanding music theorist, Sefieddin Urmavi, created a new system of musical notation. His *Treatise on Music* became a handbook for musicologists for generations. By the nineteenth century, musical development culminated in the composer Uzeir Hajibeyov's opera *Leyli ve Mejnun*. The Conservatoire in Baku has maintained high standards through many difficulties, producing composers such as Gara Garayev, Fikret Amirov, Niyazi, Arif Melikov and others. The multi-national community of Baku helped classical music to evolve and to this day accomplished performers are winning acclaim far and wide.

Uzeir Hajibeyov, composer

A traditional, Eastern form of music called *Mugam* developed in Azerbaijan with its own virtuoso performers. Some of these have gained fame through very varied forms of music. There are the examples of Jabbar Garyagdy, Bul-Bul, Reshid Behbudov and the well-known jazz musician Vagif Mustafazade.

In order to support cultural activities, every government of Azerbaijan has always attempted to maintain their institutions. There are over 100 museums and art galleries, over 4,000 public libraries (the largest being the Akhundov Library) and 25 state theatres. There are cultural centres for children and youth; several orchestras, including the Philharmonic Orchestra and the Children's Philharmonic Orchestra and several chamber orchestras.

At present there are around 40 higher education institutions, including the prestigious Baku State University. Separate but equally distinguished is the Academy of Sciences of Azerbaijan, which consists of 14 institutes. In addition, there are centres for film-making and other institutions for fine art and culture. Azerbaijan is also trying hard to rebuild its once distinguished record of sporting excellence.

opposite: Carpet weaving

above: Landscape, 'Goychai',
oil on canvas,
by S B Bakhlulzade

above left: 'Azerbaijani Family'
watercolour on paper, 1914, by
Abbas Husseyni

left: 'The Lights of Mingechaur'
oil on canvas, 1948
by M H Abdullayev

Traditions

FESTIVE DAYS

National traditions are deeply respected in Azerbaijan, particularly holidays. Some are religious, such as *Gurban-Bayram* (the Day of Sacrifice), *Orujlug* (the end of Ramadan) and *Meherremlik* (the Mourning Ritual).

Novruz Bayram (novruz means 'new day') is a widely celebrated holiday in Azerbaijan. It is an ancient public holiday of the new year and spring, celebrated at the equinox, usually on 21 March. People prepare for it well in advance, repairing their houses and apartments, sewing new clothes, painting eggs and germinating wheat on decorative plates. Various sweetmeats are prepared on the eve of the holiday, especially *govurga*, which contains sultanas and nuts, *pakhlava* and *shekerbura*. In the evening, bonfires are lit in the courtyards and children jump over them, while the adults prepare more food in the hope of a rich and fertile year ahead.

Modern, mainly Western, holidays such as New Year are also celebrated, especially in the cities, with champagne and festive foods at midnight. In rural regions, a harvest festival is also celebrated.

HANDICRAFTS

Plentiful and diverse raw resources have enabled the development of handicrafts since ancient times. These include pottery, leather and metalwork, the making of armour and textiles. Cloth has been made

Aftafalayan, water jugs for washing hands

from coarse calico, silk and wool, especially woven wool and padded silk fabric. You can still find good examples of skilfully made jewellery, carved wood, stone and metal. Enamel work is also used in jewellery.

The best known handicraft is carpet making. This art was originally developed in Guba, Shirvan, Ganja, Gazakh, Garabagh

right: Sheki,
'shebeke' wooden
ornamentation

opposite: Musical
instruments

and around Baku. These are the areas where sheep were first kept for their wool. Although traditional patterns are still used, modern carpet weavers also enjoy creating literary images and individual portraits.

Ornaments on buildings are also part of the local tradition, made of stone or wood. Windows were decorated, either with carvings

from a single piece of wood or an elaborate assemblage of delicate wooden shapes. These elegant gratings are called *shebeke*. The favourite patterns used for stone or wood carving were geometric or stylised plants. Often, these were used to decorate lavishly the interiors of the houses of the wealthy. In more recent buildings, carving and painting can be seen also, for example in the Nizami Museum and other public buildings in Baku and elsewhere.

Traditional nineteenth century dress

TRADITIONAL DRESS

Traditional clothes among Azerbaijanis changed little up to the beginning of the twentieth century. Men's dress at the time was similar to that of the rest of the Caucasus, except for minor differences in the cut and ornaments. Naturally, city-dwellers and peasants did not dress exactly the same, and neither did the rich and the poor. Peasants wore wide pantaloons with a belt made from home-spun cloth and with a simple tunic made from a variety of materials including cotton and satin, especially a woollen (occasionally silk) kaftan called an *arkhalyg*. The dress was completed with a fluffy sheep's wool hat (*papag*), woollen or silk socks and home-made, rawhide slippers. The better off wore a *chukha* (a tight fitting jacket) and a *kurk* (a sheepskin coat) in winter.

City-dwellers at the turn of the

twentieth century began wearing European style trousers, but otherwise dress remained traditional. The footwear of townsmen at this time consisted either of the traditional shoe with turned up toes or a local type of European model.

The dress of Azeri women at that time was more original and unique, and varied with social status and ethnic identity. They would wear a short waist-length tunic of calico, cotton or satin among the poor, and of silk among the rich. They also wore wide skirts gathered at the waist of the same material.

Women's hair was always hidden under a tightly bound headscarf and covered with a decorative silk shawl. Their footwear was similar to the men's. However, they also wore ornaments on their heads, hands and bosom. In those days, Azeri women did not appear on the street without their *chadra* (a large veil) and sometimes they covered their face with a light scarf called a *rubend*. When they saw strangers, village women simply covered their mouths and the lower part of their faces with a corner of their head shawl. They all wore belts, usually made of leather with coins sewn on and with a buckle made of a rough grade of silver.

Children's clothing was similar to the adult, except that it was less decorated.

FOOD

The most traditional aspect of Azerbaijani life is the food. Villagers still prefer white bread baked in a *tendir* (clay oven). Loaves that are long and thin are usually called *chorek* and the thicker, rounder ones *lavash*. A favourite dairy product, in addition to butter and cheese, is *gatyg* (thick, soured milk).

The Azeris prepare *plov*, a rice dish cooked in over one hundred

A typical feast

above: Traditional nineteenth
century costume.
Painted by G Gagarin

left: A 'Bek' of Garabagh,
nineteenth century.
Painted by G Gagarin

different ways, for all festive occasions. It is accompanied with meat, fish, vegetables and fruits. Meat dishes are prepared with chestnuts, dried apricots, sultanas and green vegetables.

Khingal, stuffed dumplings, are a regional speciality in the north-west of the country. They can be made with meat, fried onions and a dried cottage cheese called *gurut*. Stuffed vine and cabbage leaves (*dolma*) are popular, filled with lamb, rice and spices. Minced lamb is also used to stuff aubergines, tomatoes, sweet peppers and apples.

Each region has its own local dishes. In Lenkoran, for example, chicken is stuffed with nuts, jam and onions and roasted on skewers. Fish is stuffed with the same ingredients and baked in a *tendir*.

Absheron is famous for its *dushpere* (miniature raviolis) and *kutab* (thinly covered pasties). All kinds of soups are had as a first course: *kufta-bozbash* (meat balls in broth), *khamirashy* (noodle soup) and *dougha* (made with sour milk and green vegetables).

Special sweets are prepared on festive days and for family celebrations: *shekerbura*, (a cake made with nuts and sugar wrapped in fine pastry), *pakhlava*, (a lozenge-shaped short bread with nuts) and *doshab*, a preserve made from grape and mulberry syrup.

SIGNIFICANT DATES

At the present time official holidays and significant dates are celebrated which are acceptable to both traditionalists and younger generations:

1 January – New Year
20 January – Commemoration Day (of the 'Black January' tragedy)

8 March – International Women's Day

21 March – Novruz Bayram

9 May – Victory Day

28 May – Republic Day (officially called 'Day of the Revival of Azerbaijan Statehood' which commemorates the achievement of Independence in 1918)

9 October – Day of the Armed Forces of the Azerbaijan Republic

18 October – State Independence Day

12 November – Constitution Day

17 November – National Revival Day

31 December – Day of Solidarity with Azerbaijanis throughout the World

The religious holidays of Ramadan and Kurban are celebrated according to the lunar calendar.

above: Traditional
handicrafts

opposite:
Embroidery

State Administration and Political Structure

The Azerbaijan Republic (Azərbaycan Respublıkası) is a legally constituted, secular republic. The state administration is conducted through the principle of the division of powers: legislative, executive and judicial.

The President is the Head of State and implements the policies decided democratically for the exercise of executive power. The President is elected by direct vote for a period of five years. The current President is HE Mr Heydar Aliyev.

Legislative power is implemented by the Milli Mejlis (National Assembly) which is a single-house parliament consisting of 125 deputies elected for a period of five years on the basis of a combined system of first-past-the-post and proportional representation.

Following the Soviet period, democracy developed over time, with a plethora of political parties to start with (over 60 at one time) to around 30 at the present time. The names of some of the main parties are: 'New Azerbaijan', 'Istiqlal' (Party of the National Independence of Azerbaijan), 'Musavat' (a revival of the ruling party in independent Azerbaijan of 1918-1920), 'Party of the Popular Front of Azerbaijan', 'Social-Democratic Party of Azerbaijan' and others.

A Prime Minister heads the Cabinet of Ministers, an appointed body which has the main tasks of executive power. Judicial power is implemented by the three independent courts of the Azerbaijan Republic: the Constitutional Court, High Court and Economic Court.

above: President
Heydar Aliyev. Visit
to an oil rig

left: The Parliament
Building, Baku

The official language of the Azerbaijan Republic is the Azerbaijani language which is a member of the south-western, Oguz family of Turkic languages. Informally, other languages are also used such as Russian and English. Furthermore, the constitution of the Azerbaijan Republic guarantees the free use and development of the languages of all ethnic groups which can be taught in schools and used in all publications.

Freedom of religion is also enshrined in the constitution. The religion of the majority in Azerbaijan is Islam. Not much difference is made between Shia and Sunni in Azerbaijan, but formally two thirds are considered Shia and one third are Sunni. There are also centres of worship for the Russian Orthodox Church, the Armenian Gregorian Church, three Jewish synagogues, one Georgian Orthodox church, thirteen Old Believers Russian churches (locally there are those known as 'Malakan'), one Lutheran, several Baptist, one Bahai and one Hare Krishna organisation.

Civil legislation for marriage, divorce and those elements concerned with the establishing of civil society are being drafted to reflect the secular character of the Azerbaijan state.

Geographical Features

LOCATION

Azerbaijan is located in the south-eastern part of the Caucasian isthmus, with a coast of 825 kilometres along the Caspian Sea. Much of the country is mountainous. The Greater Caucasian range rises to the north, and Bazarduzu (4,480 m) is the highest peak. Below the mountains lies the Kura-Araz lowland. The Azerbaijan Republic is 86,000 square kilometres in area, including the Nakhchivan Autonomous Republic.

Azerbaijan's northern border with the Russian Federation is 390 kilometres long. The longest border is with the Republic of Armenia to the west, 1,009 kilometres long. To the north-west the border with Georgia stretches to 480 kilometres. To the south-west, in Nakhchivan, the border with the Turkish Republic is only twelve kilometres long. To the south, Azerbaijan, including Nakhchivan, has a 765 kilometre-long border with the Islamic Republic of Iran.

GENERAL PHYSICAL FEATURES

The most remarkable geographical feature of Azerbaijan is its variety. Landscapes change from the hot lowlands of the dry subtropics to everlasting snows and glaciers in the mountains. The country has nine climatic zones out of the thirteen that exist in the world. From

above: Springtime

opposite: Apricot
harvest

dry and humid subtropics to mountainous tundra, the climate itself ranges with temperatures from +45°C in the plains to -45°C in the mountains.

Some of the plains are markedly dry and there are regions where the hills are humid, with the accompanying variations in soil and vegetation.

The passage from the 'hot house' of the lowlands – semi-humid subtropics – to the eternal snow and glaciers of the mountains is a striking experience. Medium altitude and the subalpine zones of maximum humidity have allowed the splendid natural mountain forests and subalpine meadows to flourish.

Most of the flat territory of Azerbaijan consists of a semi-desert type of landscape. This covers the following areas: the southern part of the Samur-Devechi lowland, the Absheron peninsula, most of Gobustan, all the Kura-Araz lowland and part of the right bank of the Kura River from Ganja to Aghstafa. The same landscape can be traced from the northern banks of the Mingechevir Reservoir to Gobustan and down to the plain of Nakhchivan (800-1200 metres).

This area is flat, relieved only by small clusters of low foothills (in Gobustan and in the Ganja-Gazakh plain) damaged by soil erosion and so arid that locally they are called 'badlands'. Predominant soil in this type of landscape is grey earth, with saline and fragmentary meadow grey earth. Vegetation cover is poor. Yet the economic importance for Azerbaijan of this kind of landscape is considerable. For centuries, indigenous cultivation and irrigation activities have turned this region into one of intensive agricultural production. In Gobustan and south-eastern Shirvan, where there are no irrigation systems, land is extensively used as winter pasture. These activities help to overcome the disadvantages of the heavily salted soil that prevails in the region.

Hills spread from altitudes of 400-500 metres to 1400-1600 metres, from the Jeyranchel-Ajinour foothills on the south-east of the Greater Caucasus range down to below the mountains of Nakhchivan. Mountainous grey-brown, dark-chestnut, chestnut and light-chestnut soils are all to be found here.

Lowland meadow – forest and moderately dry landscapes – are typical of the Sholar Plain, the north of the Samur-Devechi lowlands and the lower area of the Alazan-Agrichay plain. These areas typically have river deposits and there are meadow and forest soils. Vegetation consists mainly of broad-leaf forests and meadows. A special type of lowland forest landscape is connected with the semi-humid subtropics of Lenkoran. Several light broad-leaf forests developed here.

Forest type landscape is widespread in mountainous altitudes from 800 metres to 2,000-2,200 metres, within low and middle mountainous zones. Here broad-leaf forests of Iberian type (oak, hornbeam, beech and chestnut) are widely spread. The eastern slopes of the Talysh mountains are mainly covered by forests of this type (locally called Girkan). Meadows and shrubs appear in large clearings. In the mountains soils are mostly red and brown and in the less mountainous areas meadows are chalky. Within the Talysh region, poorer quality mountainous-yellow earth can be observed.

Alpine meadow landscapes are to be found at heights of 2,000-3,000 metres on the narrow slopes of the high range of both the Greater and Lesser Caucasus ranges and on the gently sloping areas of the Garabagh volcanic plateau. Subalpine and alpine meadows serve as summer pastures.

Glacial landscapes can be seen on the high mountains above 3,000 metres. Here exposed rocks, screes and moraines predominate,

Folk dancing

with some permanent snow and a few individual glaciers. Ancient glacial forms of landscape are widely developed.

Economic activity throughout the ages reflected all these variations of the complex landscape of the country.

SOIL TYPES

The surface crust of volcanic, deep, sedimentary and metamorphic rocks in mountainous areas provide valuable resources such as marble, andesit-basalt, clayey shales, sandstones and limestones.

The Kur-Araz lowlands were affected by both recent and ancient alluvia of the many rivers there. These and the mountainous streams in the sloping plains have provided rocks and pebbles in the soil.

Azerbaijan's natural, semi-desert plains of the Kur-Araz lowland have poor vegetative cover and a very limited amount of precipitation. Soil formation is affected by the different levels of solutions in the soil. The dry climate sucks moisture containing dissolved salt out of the ground. The soils of these semi-deserts, therefore, are strongly salted and also lack humus because there is a lack of decomposing vegetation. Grey earth is the predominant type of soil formation, ash grey in colour. Nevertheless, some of these kinds of whitish soil are fertile, since the great number of insoluble minerals are suitable for use in irrigation.

In the regions where the brief flourishing of spring appears more colourfully, there can be a sudden surge of meadow-like vegetation. The brief growth of turf and grasses supply the soil with some humus to form grey-earth meadows. An example of this can be found in Nakhchivan. In the north of the Husar plain, however, where the climate becomes cold and there is an increase of humidity, grey-earth meadows are replaced with forest soils.

Another variety is meadow-marsh soil along the depressions formed by old riverbeds and other damp, low-lying areas with underground water. Likewise, alluvial and forest soils can be found along rivers. These alluvial soils are created when rivers overflow. It is typical for alluvial soils to have a complex structure depending on the intensity of the flooding and the saline levels of the soil.

Humid, dark grey and brown soil, or semi-desert soil which is usually saline, is found along the sloping plains to the south-east of the Greater Caucasian range.

The soil in oases shows long agricultural activity. Such areas benefited from artificial irrigation (although there has been some poor irrigation and secondary salt contamination). They were subsequently enriched with fertilisers and became an important element of the agricultural landscape long ago.

The sloping plains at the south-western foothills of the Greater Caucasus, the north-eastern foothills of the Lesser Caucasus, as well as the slopes of the foothills of Dubrar and the northern foothills of Talysh all turn into dry steppes and no longer have the semi-desert landscape of the neighbouring regions. Here are found darker coloured, chestnut and brown soils. They are quite fertile, with large areas suitable for growing cereals, cultivating gardens and vineyards.

Close by is mountainous dry steppe, and in the foothills of the Lesser Caucasus and in parts of the Ajinour foothills chestnut soils have developed. At these lower altitudes there are sparse forests which can tolerate dry conditions where before were thick forests. In these areas there are alkaline, grey-brown and pure brown types of soil. These types contain much detritus and have an undeveloped

above: Mountain scene

right: Maraza Region,
mausoleum

profile. Usually, half way up the slopes of the mountains in dry and sparse woods dark brown soil is found. In Kedebek, however, there is limestone, so a dark coloured type of soil can be observed. There are also mountain forest steppes where highly fertile, black earth can be seen.

In Talysh and particularly in the Lenkoran region an unusual type of soil is represented. There is a great deal of warmth and humidity so chemical weathering is intense here. Upper levels of insoluble, residual iron oxide and aluminium have accumulated. Because of this, the soil becomes yellowish and sometimes even bright yellow, almost orange. Tea bushes and many other subtropical crops grow well in the yellow earth of Lenkoran. On the higher slopes of Talysh, nearer the mountain peaks, the yellow earth gives way to mountain forest and dark brown soil.

Mountain-meadow soil predominates on the wide Garabagh plateau and on the mountain highlands covered in forest. There is also a certain amount of peat.

Some variations can be observed where 'slipping' occurs in high altitude soils. Thus on some northern slopes, which are usually less stony and unlike the steppes, soils can 'slip' to a lower level which is not the case on southern slopes.

CLIMATE

In the plains the summer is hot and dry, autumn is warm and rainy, winter is cool and in spring the weather is irregular. In the mountains there are strong contrasts between wind-free slopes and those exposed to sun and wind. These are the general climatic characteristics of Azerbaijan, which is basically transient to subtropical. Most of the territory of the Republic has either dry, subtropical plains or humid regions in the Alazan-Agrichay valley and the Lenkoran lowlands where subtropical crops can be grown. These climatic features are affected by the geographical location of Azerbaijan, the diversity of the soils that cover it and its weather patterns.

Atmospheric circulation over Azerbaijan is typical of a subtropical zone. One of the main features is the way air masses move, especially in the cold periods of the year. During warm periods there is usually less cloud and the weather can be markedly hot. At such times of the year winds from the mountains blow into the valleys and sometimes reach high speeds. In the plains they form light winds which become coastal breezes when they reach the sea. In summer, there is drought and the weather is hot and dry. Hot and dry winds come from continental tropical air carried from Central Asia by anti-cyclones or from the south and south-west on variable high pressure systems and these cause damage to agriculture as much as drought.

The dynamics of what is happening in the atmosphere in the cold period of the year are quite different. The territory of Azerbaijan is affected by cold fronts, which start off almost imperceptibly but which become intensively cold with Arctic air which alternates with that of more temperate latitudes.

There are polar anti-cyclones, which extend to all of Europe and the Caucasus. When these reach the subtropics they create favourable conditions for the formation of polar high-frontal zones. There is also a variable southern cyclonic weather pattern that appears in the Mediterranean and moves towards the southern Caucasus.

Frontal zones bring tropical air masses from the Atlantic and warm fronts are created in the mountains of Azerbaijan which gives

Edge of the village

a high rate of rainfall during the period between autumn and winter. Rainfall is also increased when cold fronts and anti-cyclones and southern cyclones reach the region.

The mountain system of the Caucasus has a strong influence on the general weather processes in Azerbaijan. The Greater Caucasus range stands as a natural barrier between the cold air masses from the north, and the hot tropical air from the south. This creates favourable conditions for a warm and mild climate.

Simultaneously, the complex interaction of the atmosphere with the mountain system of Azerbaijan and the Caspian Sea causes differences in the distribution of rainfall. This explains why there are different levels of rainfall in the different regions of the Republic. The intrusion of cold air masses causes unfavourable weather conditions with snowstorms and drifts and strong frosts that inconvenience the population at large. North winds can also reach hurricane strength in Baku and in the Absheron peninsula there are also strong south-westerly winds.

The highest average temperature during the year is observed in the plains of Azerbaijan, in the Kura-Araz and Lenkoran lowlands, where temperatures exceed 41°C. In the mountains the temperature drops to between 4.5°C and 6.6°C at heights of 2,000 metres. When the altitude is above 3,000 metres it can fall to –10°C.

The average temperature in January in the plains and in the foothills usually exceeds 0°C, but some falls of temperature are accompanied by strong frosts when, in the Lenkoran lowlands, the temperature can reach –13 to –17°C and elsewhere even –20°C. One can usually guess the temperature in the mountains since the temperature drops 0.5°C for each 100 metres of altitude. In this way, in both the Greater and Lesser Caucasus an altitude of 2,000 metres

Pastoral scene

Country road

would indicate that the average temperature in January is close to -5°C to -10°C at 3,000 metres.

The air gets dramatically warmer in the plains and foothills in the spring because of the dry warm winds from the Talysh mountains and the arrival of tropical air.

The hottest months are July and August. The average temperature in July is 25-27°C in the Kura-Araz plain, in the foothills to the south and west of the Absheron peninsula and in the foothills of Nakhchivan. The moderate influence of the Caspian Sea extends only to the coastal line. At different times the arrival of tropical air from the south can cause heatwaves both in the lowlands and along the Caspian. In Nakhchivan the temperature can reach 40-43°C degrees. At an altitude of 2,000 metres the average temperature in July is close to 15°C degrees; above 3,000 metres it is 3-9°C degrees and on the highest peaks can drop even below 0°C.

It is interesting that despite the proximity of a water source as large as the Caspian Sea, the main sources of humidity are the Atlantic air masses and not those of the Caspian. For example, rainfall is higher in the south-eastern end of the Greater Caucasus compared to the central region near the Kura basin.

This relationship exists despite the fact that on the Caspian coastline some monsoon circulation is observed. In summer, the cold air from the sea is drawn into the area of low pressure above the hot plains, and in winter the wind blows from the land towards the ice-free seas. But here the summer 'monsoon', as it is called, does not bring rainfall as in the Far East and South Asia.

Although the Caspian produces humid air it does not always result in high levels of precipitation. Humidity levels above the sea vary from a monthly average of eighty per cent to eighty-five per cent in the winter and drop to seventy per cent or seventy-five per cent in the summer. In the mountains the humidity index is barely seven per cent. In the regions away from the sea, relative humidity in summer is also much less than in coastal regions (average twenty per cent). Evaporation from the surface of the Caspian Sea is blown by the wind which creates humidity in the sea air along the coast and which is cold in winter.

Rainfall is unequally distributed over the territory of Azerbaijan. South of the Absheron peninsula yearly precipitation is never more than 200 mm, whereas in the south of the Lenkoran lowlands, for example, there is an annual rate of more than 1,600 mm. Most of the Kura-Araz lowlands, the Nakhchivan plain bordering the Araz, the high mountain zone in Talysh and northern Absheron all receive 200-300 mm of precipitation annually. Dew provides additional moisture in the Kura-Araz lowlands. In the sloping plains below the foothills there is an average of 300-400 mm, in the foothills in much of Nakhchivan 400-600 mm, and from 600 mm to 900 mm in central areas of the Lesser Caucasus. In the mountains of the central area of the Greater Caucasus, however, the annual index can reach 600 mm to 1,200 mm. The range's southern slopes and the centre of Lenkoran both have levels higher than 1,200 mm, and up to 1,700 mm in the far south of the Lenkoran lowlands.

Snow cover in many parts of Azerbaijan appears irregularly and in varying quantities. In all the lowlands and foothills snow does not remain long, on average less than 10-15 days per year. Snowfall stabilises only in altitudes exceeding 1,400-1,500 metres above sea level, sometimes lasting from fifty to one hundred days and for more than half a year in some places. In Nakhchivan snow remains for a long time at altitudes of 900 to 1,000 metres and above.

Occasionally there are hailstorms that damage vineyards, gardens and plantations, especially in the middle and upper mountain zones

Village view

in both Caucasian ranges and in Nakhchivan. There are between five and ten hailstorms every year in these regions. On average every thirty to forty-five days there are thunderstorms in the mountains and every five to fifteen days along the coastal plains and the Kura-Araz lowlands.

The semi-deserts and dry steppes of the Araz River zone of Nakhchivan have a cold climate in winter and hot dry summers. The climate of the forest-covered areas on the southern and north-eastern slopes of the Greater Caucasus is moderately warm with regular precipitation. Higher up, above 2,700 metres, there are cold and dry winters, as well as in the Lesser Caucasus at altitudes between 1,400 metres and 2,700 metres. There is also plenty of moisture and a moderately warm climate most of the year in the subtropical areas of the Lenkoran lowlands and the Talysh foothills. A cold climate with dry summers is typical for Nakhchivan, especially up to 1,000 metres. However, towards Zengezur and high up, between 2,700 and 3,000 metres, there is a cold and humid climate all year round.

Geology and Natural Resources

The geological structure of Azerbaijan was formed over millions of years. In the Palaeozoic and Mesozoic Ages land appeared in different shapes, often long ridges, out of the ancient seas. On the seabed, limestone, sand and clay deposits accumulated from neighbouring areas. Volcanoes spewed lava and ash which turned into hard igneous rocks. Rock deposits were transformed under the sea, sometimes into long ridges. The same transformations occurred on dry land in the mountains and valleys. Sediments were formed out of molten volcanic lava and gasses which eventually led to the deposits which characterise the area:

• a complex system of a great arch of prominent ridges (giant anticlines) in the Greater Caucasus, with the lower heights being more recent

• sinclines which enter Azerbaijan on the Husari slopes

• the valley around the Kura River between the mountains which forms a zone of deep troughs and giant sinclines where lowlands predominate

• a line of fragmented, prominent folds of the Lesser Caucasus and prominent parts of the South Caucasian plateau, with varying activity of old and new volcanoes at a lower altitude than the Greater Caucasian range

• sinclines along the line of the Araz (Nakhchivan)

Traces of the most ancient stages in the development of the earth's crust within present-day Azerbaijan have been detected from the lower Palaeozoic, when most of its territory was covered by the sea. Land existed only in the area of the present Kur depression. Marine deposits of the Palaeozoic period were to form part of the South Caucasian plateau.

The Jurassic period was marked by strong underwater volcanism. Lava and granites of that time, several kilometres deep, came to form the highest point in the north-east of the Lesser Caucasus, particularly the Murovdag and Garabagh mountain peaks. Above the surface of the sea, chains of volcanic islands appeared.

These island ridges appeared and disappeared again and again depending on the sea level, but later they were to remain as permanent cores around which land grew. The surrounding seas gradually divided into separate narrow basins. Nearly the entire territory of the future Azerbaijan, except for an archipelago of rocky islands, sank into the expanding waters, after which there was no further change.

Beginning from the Cenozoic period the landscape of Azerbaijan began to be transformed. Areas of land below the surface and what were previous marine inlets in the territory of the Greater and Lesser Caucasus began not only to dry out but also became a nucleus for the growth of land and the creation of mountains. What had previously existed was completely transformed. Eventually both Caucasian ranges rose out of the sea. In some of the mountains and in Talysh, one can still see traces of earlier types of surface structures.

The Greater and Lesser Caucasus and Talysh were transformed into real mountain systems with deep river valleys. Within the South Caucasian plateau very intensive volcanism appeared. Volcanic

A river in the
mountains

Mountain viewing-
point

basaltic lavas were poured out, volcanic domes and cones were formed (Great Ishikhly, Ginaldag, etc). In the clay and sand at the foot of the mountains rich oil resources accumulated.

The sea gradually retreated and the maritime plains emerged. The network of river systems, similar to the present Kur and Araz river systems, was established. As the land rose, valleys with rivers cut in deeper into the earth and terraces appeared within them. Coastal terraces formed as well. Land movement along with climatic factors contributed further to the lowering of the level of the future Caspian Sea.

After the ice ages with the warming and drying up of the climate, the number of mountainous glaciers decreased and most of them disappeared. In Azerbaijan only a number of small glaciers survived on the highest peaks of the Greater and Lesser Caucasus.

Thus the diverse, beautiful and varied landscape of modern Azerbaijan was established.

Along the crest of the south-eastern part of the Greater Caucasus runs the border of Azerbaijan with the Russian Federation (with Dagestan). In the north-west of the Republic this peak falls very steeply towards the Alazan-Agrichay valley.

To the east of Bazarduzu (4,466 metres) there is the highest peak of all the Eastern Caucasus and both of the slopes are part of Azerbaijan.

To the east and south-east of Babadag, the Greater Caucasus falls away sharply and becomes a middle altitude mountain area, often named Dubrar. On the south-east it is joined by the hilly ridges and low mountains of Gobustan and on the east they are joined by the plains and low plateau of the Absheron peninsula. Both of these areas have a great number of active mud volcanoes.

The Kur valley belongs almost wholly within Azerbaijan, with the exception of its north-western part, which forms part of Georgia. This narrow north-western part is divided by the Middle Kur highlands into two plains, the Alazan-Alachay in the north and the Ganja-Gazakh in the southwest. The Kur-Araz lowland occupies the centre and like the Caspian lies below mean sea level. It is framed by low, arid mountains and sloping plains. In the west, in the foothills of the Lesser Caucasus, it is joined by the Garabagh and Mil plains and in the north in the foothills of the Greater Caucasus by the Shirvan plain. The banks of the Araz and lower Kur form part of the Mugam plain of Iran to the south. The Salyan plain which is situated on the right bank and south-eastern Shirvan which is situated on the left bank lie at the estuary of the Kur river. The flat landscape is relieved only by small hills (*tepe*) and hillocks near the Kur and Araz rivers. On the coast chains of volcanic mud islands, the Absheron archipelago near the Absheron peninsula and the Baku archipelago on the coast of Gobustan and the Kur-Araz lowland, rise out of the waters of the Caspian. Recently, artificial chains of islands, such as Oily Rocks and others, built by man for the extraction of oil from the Caspian Sea, contrast with the natural ones.

The south-eastern part of the Lesser Caucasus is located within Azerbaijan. This system consists of a number of high altitude peaks and a great number of middle altitude and low altitude spurs. The valley of the Terter river divides the Azerbaijani part of the Lesser Caucasus into two parts, north-western and south-eastern. The first is created by the gentle slope of two peaks, Shahdag with the Ginaldag peak (3,367 metres), and the latter, the Murovdag, with the Gyamysh peak (3,724 metres). Both slopes of Murovdag are part of Azerbaijan and the border between Azerbaijan and Armenia lies along the watershed of the Shahdag crest. In the south-east of the Lesser Caucasus the peak of Garabagh rises with the Beyuk-Kirs

above: Baku on the
Caspian coast

opposite: 'Istiglal'
oil rig

peak (2,725 metres). It is situated above the Garabaghi plain and in the neighbourhood of the city of Khankendi. In the south the mountains become the Geyan steppe divided by hills from the plains situated on the left bank of the Araz.

The inland region of the South Caucasian plateau extends into Armenia and Georgia. It touches Azerbaijan in two small areas that are divided by the territory of Armenia. To the east of this projection is the Garabaghi volcanic plateau. Some peaks reach more than 3,000 metres (Ishighly mountain, 3,552 metres) but mostly the average altitude is 1,500-2,500 metres. In the north-west the eastern Sevan crest which borders Armenia separates the Garabagh plateau from the Sevan valley.

On the territory of the Nakhchivan Autonomous Republic of the Azerbaijan Republic, up near the Araz plain of Nakhchivan, which occupies the left bank of the Araz, is Zengezur. On the west by the Daralagez border are high peaks.

The peak of the Zengezur crest, Mount Kapujukh (3,904 metres), is the highest non–volcanic peak of all the South Caucasian plateau. The deep ravine of the Araz winds along the southern foothills of the Zengezur crest.

The Talysh mountains rise to medium altitudes and their highest peak is Mount Kumurkey (2,477 metres). The north-eastern slopes which form the greater part of these mountains are divided by valleys into three parallel chains. These are within Azerbaijan and the rest in Iran, separated by the waters that form the border.

opposite:
**Archeological finds
in the Caspian**

NATURAL RESOURCES

Azerbaijan is very rich in natural resources, the most important being oil, with most of the famous oil fields situated in the Absheron peninsula, offshore and onshore. These are discussed more fully below in the section on the economy. Gas too has been discovered and there are also sources of medicinal oil, called 'Naphtalan', which are unique, located near the city of Ganja.

Minerals include iron ore, alunites, sulphuric pyrites, molybdenum and arsenic. Other metal ores have been found in Fizilchay.

There is iron ore in Dashkesan in the Lesser Caucasus, and in nearby Zaglik is one of the largest known reserves of alunites from which aluminium is made. Cobalt and sulphuric pyrites can be mined in the same region. Rock salt, arsenic ores and molybdenum can be mined in Paragachay in Nakhchivan.

There is also marble and granite in the Lesser Caucasus, and gravel, limestone and fire-resistant brick clay in Absheron. Well-known mineral waters which arise from volcanic and limestone rocks come from Istisu, Turshsu and Badamly.

As we have already noted, the surface of Azerbaijan consists of a flat area surrounded by steep mountains which slope towards the Caspian Sea and some isolated plains. The mountains provide barriers from the northern winds and the humidity from the west. They also moderate the humidity from the Caspian Sea. Only from the north-east and east is Azerbaijan open to the intrusion of air masses from near the region of the Urals, Siberia and Central Asia.

These major features and Azerbaijan's geographical location

determine its natural habitat, which differs from that of other countries located on the same latitudes.

Although there are some pockets of desert and steppe which resemble those of Central Asia they can be crossed in less than three hours driving and there is dense forest in the surrounding mountains. Vegetation is more tolerant of dry conditions on the edges of the Greater and Lesser Caucasus. On the mountain slopes where there are few trees some cultivation is possible.

A great number of rivers flow from the mountains to the plains and fan out to create 'dry deltas' in the foothills, in a line of oases. It is not by accident that most of the cities and villages of Azerbaijan are situated in this zone. Here there is plenty of water for gardens, plantations, vegetable plots, vineyards, and trees such poplars, walnut trees, plane trees and others.

CASPIAN SEA

The Caspian Sea is the largest salt lake in the world. But its size, hydrologic characteristics and origin also provide the reasons for it to be called a sea. It is thought that in the past, the Caspian was linked to larger seas in the west and the north. The past connection with northern seas can be seen through the palaeontological data of some types of animal forms preserved in the Caspian (up to fifteen types of crustacea and fishes and other representatives of cold water fauna).

The total area of the Caspian is 394,000 square kilometres and therefore larger than some seas. The volume of water is 76,000 cubic kilometres. The length of the coastline is approximately 6,380 kilometres of which 800 are in Azerbaijan. The northern coast of Azerbaijan borders the Middle Caspian and the Southern Caspian in the south-east. These two areas are divided by a marine ridge which is a continuation of the mountain system of both Caucasian mountain ranges and the Absheron peninsula. In 1862 the expedition of N Ivashnikov came to the conclusion that the Caspian's shallower part was 185 metres deep and the depths adjoining to the north were 500-600 metres deep. The deepest section in the Derbent trough of the Middle Caspian was 760 metres, whereas the Lenkoran trough was 1,020 metres deep.

Surface and underground outflows, together with atmospheric precipitation, fill the Caspian Sea with water at an annual rate of approximately 417 cubic kilometres. The same amount evaporates from the surface. The sea level changes when this balance is not achieved. The present level of the sea is 28 metres lower than mean sea level, but this fluctuated greatly in the past. There is evidence for this from historical documents, archaeological ruins and coastal terraces.

The level of the Caspian Sea is changing at present, as well. This affects the development of many of branches of the economy, for example, maritime transport, the oil industry and fishing. During the past forty years the level of the Caspian Sea has fallen by 2.5 metres. One reason for this is global warming; there is also the increase in the use of river water for industrial needs and some changes may have been due to tectonic factors. Annual variations are between 0.5 metres and 0.6 metres. The level rises despite strong evaporation in summer. The Bay of Baku can be affected through the differences in pressure affecting the winds over the sea giving variations of 0.7 to 0.8 metres.

The temperature of the water also changes significantly according to the season and the area of the sea. The average

temperature in summer varies from 22°C degrees along the north coast of Azerbaijan to 26°C degrees in the south. In winter the water can fall to 5°C degrees in the north to 8°C degrees in the south. Salt levels in the Middle and Southern Caspian vary between 11-13 per cent and drop to nearly 0 per cent near river estuaries.

The colour of water changes from blue-green in the open seas to dark brown near the coast and especially near the rivers, which also affect the degree of clarity. Currents depend on wind speeds and they can reach 1.5 to 2 metres per second.

Oily Rocks

Storms in the north cause waves of 9 to 10 metres high and 14 to 15 metres where there is no influence from the land mass. The Absheron coast with its frequent storms is often thought to be among the most difficult for navigation and hydro-technical construction work.

Only the northern part of the Caspian Sea freezes in winter and this does not affect Azerbaijan except sporadically at the end of winter (February). But in abnormally cold years, ice is driven from the north by winds and currents up to Absheron and they threaten the oil fields and platforms in the sea. The formation of local ice, 20-25 cm thick, has been also observed here.

Azerbaijan's north-eastern sea coast is almost straight, with hardly any indentations at all. Only the Absheron peninsula stands out into the sea for approximately 70 kilometres and with a width of around 35 kilometres.

Further south the coast is more indented. Capes, bights, bays and archipelagos have been formed because the coastline was susceptible to tectonic changes. Mud volcanism is active here too. The coast sinks into the water and again islands and even ruins of human settlements arise from the waters.

There are ancient legends of sunken cities in the Caspian Sea and about a neck of land which once connected the western and eastern sea coasts. Yunan-Sheher ('City of the Greeks') was the name given to a supposed city close to Baku and now popularly presumed to be submerged under the Caspian waters.

Another city which is described in ancient times is on an island off the Kura River estuary, 'Devil's Settlement', mentioned by the Arab geographer Istakhri (951-1000 AD). This name also appeared on an 1825 map for a nearby island.

In May 1861 an island appeared near Kumani shoal as a result of an eruption. It had disappeared by the beginning of 1862 and research indicated it arose again as a shoal in 1869. It arose and disappeared again, even in the past ten years. Could this have been the legendary sunken island? Even today fishermen and navigators call this area Kharaba-Shekher ('Ruins of the City'). In the Caspian Sea there is evidence of permanent tectonic activity with underwater mud volcanoes and earthquakes (for example, that of 27 January 1963), which may partly explain some of its history.

The Caspian Sea is crucial to Azerbaijan as a transport route and a source of different salts and, of course, the oil and gas from the seabed.

Vineyards

Economy

NATURAL RESOURCES

Azerbaijan, through its natural resources and conditions, is potentially one of the wealthiest countries in the region and, if measured by its potential per capita income, perhaps could be among the richest in the world.

Energy resources constitute its major natural asset. According to estimates, the country's oil reserves vary between 6 (proven) and up to 50 billion barrels (potential). Natural gas reserves amount to over 1200 billion cubic metres (bcm) with potential new discoveries greatly exceeding estimated reserves.

Other natural minerals include: ferrous and non-ferrous metals, e.g. alumina, alunite, gold, iron ore, lead, zinc, arsenic, copper, molybdenum, as well as salt, construction materials such as limestone, bitumen, fire clay, marble and others. The country is also rich in sources of natural mineral waters, some with unique medicinal qualities.

Azerbaijan is a country with enormous agricultural potential due to its favourable climate, fertile lands, and with the necessary diversity to enable the cultivation of a wide range of crops.

Historical and natural attractions, national cuisine, traditions and culture create favourable conditions for the development of tourism.

Its important geographical location at the cross-roads linking the two major economic power centres of Europe and Asia, as well as a key position on the Caspian Sea, will undoubtedly serve the interests of economic development in Azerbaijan as well as other countries of the region.

The comparative advantages mentioned above, together with young, dynamic but low cost labour resources make the country one of the most attractive for foreign co-operation and potentially one of the most dynamic for development.

SECTORAL BREAKDOWN OF GROSS DOMESTIC PRODUCT

Azerbaijan is an agro-industrial country with a relatively equal division between the two sectors of the economy as expressed in its gross domestic product (GDP). Industry constitutes up to 25 per cent of GDP and 20 per cent of employment. However, with an extensive oil sector, its development share of the industry in GDP

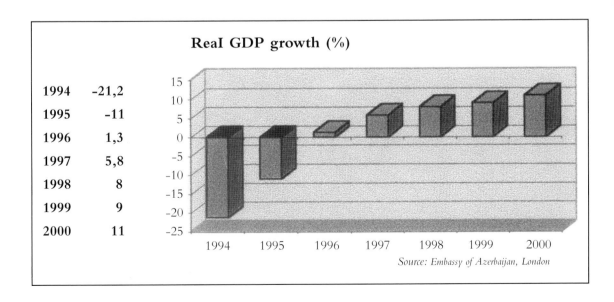

Real GDP growth (%)

1994	-21,2
1995	-11
1996	1,3
1997	5,8
1998	8
1999	9
2000	11

Source: Embassy of Azerbaijan, London

will grow permanently. Agriculture, however, remains a significant sector, constituting up to thirty per cent of GDP and employing about forty per cent of labour. Construction, transport, communications and other services make up another important part of the economy.

More than half of the industrial production is concentrated in the Absheron peninsula, around the capital city Baku and its industrial satellite Sumgait. Since the 1970s, measures have been taken, however, to distribute more evenly the geographical location of new industrial developments.

PUBLIC VERSUS PRIVATE SECTOR

After gaining independence in 1991, Azerbaijan endorsed market principles in its new Constitution, as the only possible alternative to capitalise on the country's geographical and natural comparative advantages. Private initiative and private ownership are now the main founding principles and driving force for future progress. As a result of the reforms, the private sector currently accounts for about half of the GDP and over 50 per cent of employment.

INDUSTRY

Dynamic development of Baku as a major regional, industrial centre began at the end of the last century with extensive exploration and development of its oil wealth. Since the beginning of this century Azerbaijan experienced several waves of industrialisation, first closely linked with the development of its oil sector and infrastructure.

opposite: Upgrading a drilling rig

Azerbaijan: Country Presentation   **Embassy of Azerbaijan, London**
Source: ASSC

Selective Industrial Indicators

	1990	1994
Gross industrial output index (1990 = 100)	100	38
Production of selected manufactured goods:		
Electricity, B kWh	23.2	17.6
Petroil, M ton	12.5	9.6
Gas, bn cub. M	9.9	6.4
Refrigerators, ('000)	330	97
Air conditioners, ('000)	309	119
Caustic soda, ('000 t)	160	40
Sulphuric acid, ('000 t)	603	56
Pure cotton, ('000 t)	167	74
Footwear, M pairs	15	3
All kinds of cloths, M cub. m	151	85
Mineral water, M liter	162	2
Grape wine, ('000 dl)	9,362	1,008
Champagne, ('000 dl)	1,362	270
Cognac, ('000 dl)	1,771	407

Since the 1960s the emphasis was on the diversification of its industrial structure with many new manufacturing industries being developed such as electronics, electromechanics, engineering, machinery, consumer durables, metallurgy and so on.

Nowadays, the strategy of the industrial development of the country is to serve the strengthening of its political and economic independence. The current wave of industrialisation aims at reviving its oil industry on a technologically modern base as a major driving force of economic development. The emphasis is on an industrial sector that is competitive, self-sustained and self-sufficient, balanced and harmoniously integrated into a new regional and international context based on its comparative advantages.

ENERGY

Oil wealth is one of the main strategic, natural assets which played a significant role in the history of the country and its economic development.

As has already been stated, Azerbaijan is often referred to as 'the land of fire', since ancient religions based on fire worshipping originated in this land. Among the first written sources referring to the Baku oil were those of Marco Polo, who travelled along the ancient Silk Road.

The fame of Baku's oil riches spread over the world and attracted a flow of foreign investors as the industrial revolution gained its momentum. First industrial development of the Absheron oilfields began in the middle of the last century. In 1848 the first derrick in the world was installed in Azerbaijan and in 1871 the country witnessed the first use of a steam engine in oil production. At the

Shipbuilding

turn of the century Azerbaijan was producing over half of the world's oil. Baku was therefore widely recognised as the cradle of the oil industry, and it was turned into one of the most vibrant and dynamic industrial centres of the times. Such prominent names as Nobel, Rothschild, Samuel, Rockefeller and others made their fortunes by contributing to the development of the local industry, as has already been mentioned.

Dynamic development of the oil industry, as well as the ever growing world demand for oil and the necessity for its transportation to international markets, was accompanied by such technological innovations as the world's first oil tanker, and one of the first industrial pipelines connecting the Caspian and Black Seas. In 1924 the first offshore well was drilled, thus pioneering offshore explorations.

Keeping up with its innovative traditions, in 1949 offshore developments expanded further into the open seas, resulting in the erection of the world's first and largest 'town' on rigs, known as Oily Rocks.

When talking about the history of the oil industry in Azerbaijan one cannot avoid mentioning that Baku oil played a crucial role in defeating German fascism, when every second Soviet combat tank and every two out of three war planes were fuelled by this oil. It is understandable why Baku was one of the prime targets in Hitler's plan in defeating the Soviet Union.

The rest of the Soviet period of the oil industry can be characterised by a neglectful attitude to further oil exploration and development as new oilfields were discovered in Western Siberia. However, Azeri oil engineers and specialists played an important role in discovering and developing new oilfields in Russia, in other republics of the former Soviet Union, countries of the

Middle East, North Africa and South-East Asia.

According to experts' rough estimates, over six bn barrels of oil have been extracted so far from Azeri onshore and offshore fields. Despite the barbaric and neglectful exploitation of local oilfields, most reserves still remain untapped.

As stated above, proven recoverable oil reserves in Azerbaijan are about six-seven bn barrels. Estimated total reserves are over thirty bn barrels. There are sixty-seven discovered oilfields in Azerbaijan of which only forty-four are currently operating. More than 75 per cent of its oil resources are offshore.

The new era in the reviving of the country's oil industry started in the early 1990s with the independence of Azerbaijan. Resisting all internal and external pressures, the leadership of Azerbaijan opened the riches of the Caspian Sea to the international community by inviting oil majors in developing its reserves.

On 20 September 1994 the 'Contract of the Century' was signed between the Government of Azerbaijan and a number of oil companies for the development of the prospective 'Azeri', 'Chirag' and 'Gunashli' oilfields. According to this contract over half a billion tons of oil will be developed. This agreement is being successfully implemented.

Since this first international contract, just within five years another nineteen production-sharing agreements (PSAs) worth over US$40bn have been signed with leading international oil companies to develop offshore and onshore fields. A number of new PSAs are awaiting the ceremonies to mark their signing. Such international oil companies as Agip, Amoco, BP-Amoco, Chevron, Elf, Exxon, Pennzoil, Ramco, Shell, Texaco, Total and many others, representing over 14 nations, are now established in Baku, thus turning the capital of Azerbaijan into a truly United Nations of the Oil Industry.

opposite: Industrial installation

Peak oil production is expected to be reached by 2010 at the level of 45-50 million tonnes a year (currently just over 11 Million tonnes).

Baku again, as a century ago, is on track to revive itself as a major oil centre in the new global oil province around the Caspian Sea.

The New Oil Boom

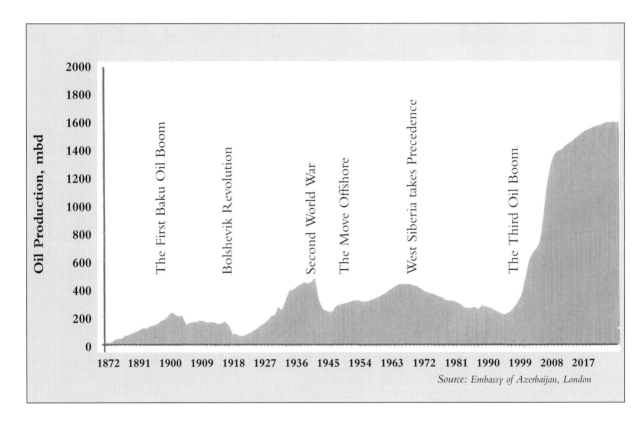

Source: Embassy of Azerbaijan, London

OIL RELATED INDUSTRY

Extensive oil exploration led to the creation of a huge industrial complex to serve the developments around the Caspian and parts of the former USSR. Over 20 large enterprises, employing 20,000 people, satisfied up to 70 per cent of the needs of the whole USSR in special equipment and machinery. Produce ranges included industrial pumping units, submersible oil pumps, drilling rigs, offshore platforms, well installations, water and gas taps, derricks and so on. The largest offshore platform production plant in Europe was put into operation in the early 1980s. Nowadays, the industry is targeting itself to serve massive developments of energy resources in the Caspian region as well as in other oil provinces. At present, the industry is in desperate need of restructuring and modernisation and to switch production to internationally acceptable engineering standards.

GAS

Azerbaijani gas reserves are estimated at about 1,500 billion cubic metres (bcm). However, with further oil exploration potential gas reserves in the offshore fields appear to be much more significant. This means that alongside oil exports, Azerbaijan may become a significant gas exporter as well. Currently most of the natural gas production comes as associated gas from offshore oilfields. But there are prospects of large gas fields as well. Top levels of gas production in the Republic were about twelve bcm; current gas production decreased to about six bcm. Projected production, however, will increase up to twenty bcm by 2010. So the share of gas in the energy balance of the country will increase significantly.

REFINING, PETROCHEMICALS AND CHEMICALS

Refining capacities constitute about 23 million tonnes per year, but are currently running at about 9–10 million tonnes.

The large petrochemical and chemical industry which was established in Azerbaijan was concentrated mainly in the town of Sumgait, located north of Baku. This industry is also in need of foreign investments, modern technology and management. Its production range includes synthetics, rubber, detergents and polymeric building materials.

Sumgait is likewise a centre of metallurgy with large enterprises such as an aluminium smelter, a steel tube-rolling plant, pipe manufacturing units and so on.

There is also a wide range of items produced in Azerbaijan. The list is varied and long, including caustic soda, detergents, oxygen and acetylene, bromine, iodine, fibreglass, polyethylene and plastic materials, pharmaceuticals, tyres, alcohol, sulphuric acid, caustic potassium, synthetic and isopropyl alcohol, sylphanol, synthetic resins, just to mention a few.

POWER SECTOR

Industrialisation of the country stipulated the development of the electricity production sector. The total capacity of electric power stations is 5,000 MW, capable of producing over 23 bn KWh. However, eighty-two per cent of the production capacity was

Baku, busy city

based on thermal sources, depending mainly on oil related products. Plans are currently being discussed to develop electricity production. These are being designed to rationalise the use of energy sources by reducing the share of fuel and increasing utilisation of natural gas and hydro sources. Large hydropower projects are currently under implementation with the participation of the World Bank, EBRD, OECF of Japan and the Islamic Development Bank. A number of power plant projects based on the utilisation of accompanying gas are under consideration with the support of the Japanese government and international organisations.

MINING AND METALLURGY

The development of metallurgy in Azerbaijan was also closely connected with supplying the needs of the oil industry. The largest enterprises of the industry are a steel-rolling mill in Sumgait, an ore concentration industrial complex in Dashkesan, the Ganja alumina and Sumgait aluminium smelters as well as the Filizchay non-ferrous mining and production capacities. They play a significant role in the economy as well.

Azerbaijan was one of the four aluminium producers in the former USSR. Such products as ingots, rods, utensil and refrigerator evaporators have been produced at the Sumgait smelter from primary and secondary aluminium, but now await further development.

Significant gold reserves in the Kelbadjar region in the west of the country provide good opportunities for the diversification of the mining industry. A joint venture with a US company has been set up to tackle this challenge.

MANUFACTURING

Because of the division of labour during the Soviet era and dependency on Moscow, finished products constitute about a third of industrial production, whilst the rest is raw materials and semi-finished products. This provides great opportunities for foreign investors as manufacturing industries gain dynamism and enjoy support from the government. They constitute about twenty per cent of the total industrial output of the country. Production range varies from petrochemicals, chemicals, mechanical engineering, radio-electronics to the production of white consumer durables, such as refrigerators, air-conditioners and others.

CONSTRUCTION MATERIALS

Production of construction materials is based on remarkable resources of natural stone and limestone and is represented by the manufacturing of cement, brick, decorative tiles, window glass, and others.

LIGHT INDUSTRY

Light industries in the country are quite diverse and based on the rich natural and agricultural resources. They include cotton-spinning, textiles, sewing, wool-spinning, knitting, leather processing, footwear production, ceramics, glass and china ware.

Traditionally, Azerbaijan is a textile producer. The industry, however, utilises only a minor portion of the country's cotton

Cotton production

output. There are four major textile enterprises but the government envisages further development of the industry through the construction of new cotton spinning mills. This industry is currently experiencing reorganisation and privatisation and new enterprises are developing with intensive foreign direct investment. This industry has large export potential.

Silk production is one of the oldest traditions, with roots going back to the ancient days of the great Silk Road. Modern silk manufacturing capacities were developed in the country, to make it

below: Gathering silk cocoons

an important export item. This too is a sector hoping to benefit from new investment and development as soon as possible.

Clothing and footwear industries have large capacities in need of modernisation.

Traditional craft industries, such as the manufacturing of carpets, jewellery, copperware and others associated with Azerbaijan, are well known far beyond its borders. Different schools of carpet making were well established in Azerbaijan for centuries and are acknowledged worldwide with many of the finest pieces exhibited in leading museums throughout the world.

Traditional industries play an important role in developing rural industries and provide local employment as well as contributing to the development of tourism.

TRANSPORT AND COMMUNICATIONS

Azerbaijan has a reasonably well developed and diversified transport system and relevant infrastructure as all kinds of transport were developed in Azerbaijan. The country, however, desperately needs to upgrade its infrastucture and design and to develop in a way that could facilitate the country's closer and more balanced integration into the regional and international economy. New infrastructure is required particularly because of the oil developments in the Caspian region to export resources to international markets.

Proper and adequate development of a telecommunications system is one of the top priorities of the Government. A number of ventures have been established in this sector with companies from the UK, US, Sweden, France, Germany, Turkey and others.

AIR TRANSPORT

The history of civil aviation in Azerbaijan covers over 50 years. Initially part of a local branch of Aeroflot, the country's Civil Aviation Authority has developed into one of the largest in the former USSR, with local airlines among its leaders. They operate flights to more than a hundred destinations.

The airport at Baku has been developed to respond to the new situation with a modern cargo terminal to handle increasing cargo freight.

Azerbaijan Airlines flies to Iran, Turkey, Israel, China, Pakistan, the UK, Greece, UAE, and many other destinations in Russia and other CIS countries. Alongside market reforms, air transport was opened for private initiatives also and nowadays a number of successful local private aviation companies operate locally and internationally.

The presence of other international airlines has transformed the character of Baku's airport. British Airways, Lufthansa, Swissair, Turkish Airlines, United Arab Airlines, KLM and other international companies operate direct flights to Baku.

Without proper diversified land infrastructure, moreover, linking Azerbaijan to international markets, transportation of cargo by air continues to play an increasing role. There is the hope that there will be development of communications along the transcontinental transport corridor linking Europe with the Far East, by land and sea, so that the share of other types of transport will increase.

RAILWAYS

Azerbaijan has developed a branch railway network and infrastructure. The total length of railways is 2,200 Km. A significant portion of rail links is electrified. The rail connection between Baku and the industrial centre of Sumgait, built in 1954, was the first electrified link in the former USSR.

Railways were formerly a major form of transport in Azerbaijan with the largest share in passenger and cargo transportation. After the break up of the USSR and of the economic ties with its markets, the role of the railways significantly diminished and lost out to road transport. However, with the restoration of the Silk Road Project, modern railways undoubtedly will play a significant part. Industry is in desperate need of capital investments for its modernisation. This would be appropriate since railway tracks link the Caspian and Black Seas and provide routes into Russia and Iran. Through Georgia there are railway and highway routes into Turkey which are important to serve Azerbaijan's passenger and cargo requirements.

MARITIME TRANSPORT

This is now important for international trade. The main port of Baku facilitates transport throughout the Caspian and up the Volga River. Ferry services to Turkmenistan guarantee direct cargo transportation between the two republics, thus reviving the role of the Caucasus route as a key transit route from Europe to Asia.

Baku is the major port on the Caspian Sea.

MOTORWAYS AND ROADS

Networks are also quite extensive, exceeding 25,000 kilometres. Major arteries are hard surfaced. Road transport is witnessing dynamic development after independence following the disruption of economic ties with former markets and reflecting new development patterns. Road transport will significantly increase its share in cargo and passenger transportation as well as in servicing international cargo flows.

PIPELINE INFRASTRUCTURE

The famous Baku–Batoum pipeline built in 1900 has been renovated and brings early oil from the new offshore exploration in the Caspian through Supsa in Georgia towards the oil markets of the rest of the world.

The development of an adequate export pipeline infrastructure is crucial for the future of the country and the whole Caspian region.

The first oil pipeline to export recent Azeri oil is one running north through Russia to the Black Sea port of Novorossiysk and has been operating since 1997.

Second is the western pipeline which goes through Georgia to the Black Sea terminal at Supsa. It was commissioned in April 1999.

Both projects are to handle the volumes of the so called Early Oil phase of exploration. However, routes for the export to international markets of major volumes of oil not only from Azerbaijan but from the Caspian region as a whole are still to be decided. The optimum is for multiple pipelines in the future, with the first one running to a large and sophisticated Mediterranean oil terminal at Ceyhan in Turkey.

TOURISM

Given its attractive and advantageous geographical location, favourable weather conditions, diversity of natural and historic sites, Azerbaijan offers exciting opportunities for the development of the tourism industry. Baku and surrounding historical cities in the Absheron peninsula make Baku one of the most attractive and evocative locations of the Caspian region.

Mountains, beaches, forests and historical sites going back to the first millennium BC and even into the prehistoric period, will eventually attract many visitors.

AGRICULTURE AND FOOD

Due to the diversity of favourable bio-climatic conditions and fertile soils agriculture in Azerbaijan is of enormous potential. It enables the development of all branches of agriculture and cultivation of a wide variety of crops, including fruit and vegetables. Farming in Azerbaijan is supported by developed irrigation systems and over eighty per cent of arable lands are irrigated.

During the Soviet era with its policy for the division of labour, the agriculture of Azerbaijan came to specialise in the production of a limited number of major commercial crops, such as cotton, grapes, early fruits and vegetables to supply to the whole Soviet market for

opposite: Fruits of the harvest

further processing in other republics. After the break-up of the USSR, the major task is to diversify production to make the country self-sufficient in major crops, develop local value-added processing facilities and increase export potential.

The country is potentially self-sufficient in agricultural and food produce with still significant export potential. The sector is currently undergoing radical reorganisation with the emphasis put on private ownership and farms.

With radical steps in increasing agricultural production, the need for supporting infrastructure will grow (storage, processing and packaging facilities).

Crop growing is the leading branch and occupied by cereals, such as wheat, barley, maize and also the favourite Azerbaijani food – rice. As well as such crops a great variety of vegetables and fruits, including rare 'feihoa' fruit are produced.

Among industrial crops there are cotton, valuable types of tobacco, tea and sunflowers.

Sericulture (silk production) is one of the traditional specialisations of certain rural parts in north-west Azerbaijan.

Horticulture is developed along the sea coast of the Republic where there is a series of vegetable-growing regions, and Lenkoran specialises in early kinds of vegetables. There are unique nut plantations and mulberry trees. More than 200 types of industrial, table and sultana varieties of grapes are known in Azerbaijan. They are cultivated in the Kur-Araz lowland, the mountainous parts of Shirvan, Garabagh and Nakhchivan.

Production of major crops

(in thousand tonnes, based on average figures of the 1980s)

grain	1,400	potatoes	185
grapes	2,000	tobacco	55
cotton	830	tea	30
vegetables	860	sugar beet	28
fruits	410	vegetable oil	41

The country was one of the principal producers of wines and spirits in the former USSR.

Livestock breeding is traditionally an important branch of the agriculture of Azerbaijan. Livestock numbers are beef cattle 850,000; cows 730,000; sheep and goats 4,700,000; pigs 30,000; poultry 8,200,000; horses 38,000. This branch has great potential for development as well.

Being dependent on the supplies of meat and meat products during the Soviet era, Azerbaijan reached self-sufficiency shortly after its privatisation of livestock.

Fishing The country is one of the few in the world producing black caviar and exclusive kinds of fish (sturgeon) only available in the Caspian Sea. The Azerbaijani sector of the Caspian is the major fishing area for the famous Caspian herring. Mountain rivers provide tourist attractions to the adventurous.

The **food industry** developed evenly throughout the country and manufactures nearly all known types of products. Together with

above: Wine vaults

opposite: Grape
harvest

traditional flour-grinding, butter and cheese production and canning, other areas stand out such as winemaking (some ten types of wine, brandy and sparkling wine are manufactured in Azerbaijan), fish processing (caviar from sturgeon) and also tea and tobacco products. All have won world recognition.

ECONOMIC POLICY

Formerly as part of the USSR economy, Azerbaijan had been allocated the role of supplier of predominantly raw materials and products with no proper value added production. Currently the economy of independent Azerbaijan is undergoing major restructuring and reorganisation towards self-sufficient and self-sustainable development, integrated into the international economy.

Market reforms, because of the burdens of the Mountainous Garabagh conflict and subsequent social and political pressures, were mostly delayed till 1995, later than in other transitional economies. But measures undertaken proved to be successful in ensuring macroeconomic stability, attraction of foreign investments and the stepping up of economic growth. For example, the growth rate in 1996 was 1.3 per cent, in 1997, 5.8 per cent, and in 1998, 8.8 per cent.

Inflation rates have been curbed at around 0 to 1 per cent during last the two years of the millennium, from hyper-inflation exceeding 1,600 per cent in 1994 (to 3.4 per cent in 1997 and 0.2 per cent in 1998).

NATIONAL CURRENCY

The *manat*, introduced in 1992, due to tough monetary policy since 1995, has started to increase in value against the dollar and is considered as one of the most stable among transition economies. National reserves are at a comfortable level exceeding the level of six months of imports.

The *foreign trade regime* and domestic prices have been liberalised. Small-scale *privatisation* has been completed. Restructuring of the banking sector is underway with supervision strengthened. A new *tax code* is soon to be introduced and a treasury system has been introduced to improve expenditure management, putting the financial system on a sound footing.

PRIVATISATION

Massive privatisation, agrarian reform and reorganisation of management are the main drives in economic development. Privatisation is one of the major priorities of the Government to ensure the success of market reforms and economic development. The first stage of privatisation has recently been successfully completed with over 21,000 small, and about a thousand medium-scale, enterprises privatised.

Due to the political and economic stability which has been achieved and the commitment of the Government to market reforms, Azerbaijan is considered one of the most attractive countries for foreign investments.

Recent macroeconomic indicators are quite encouraging: the exchange rate of the national currency has been stable for nearly two

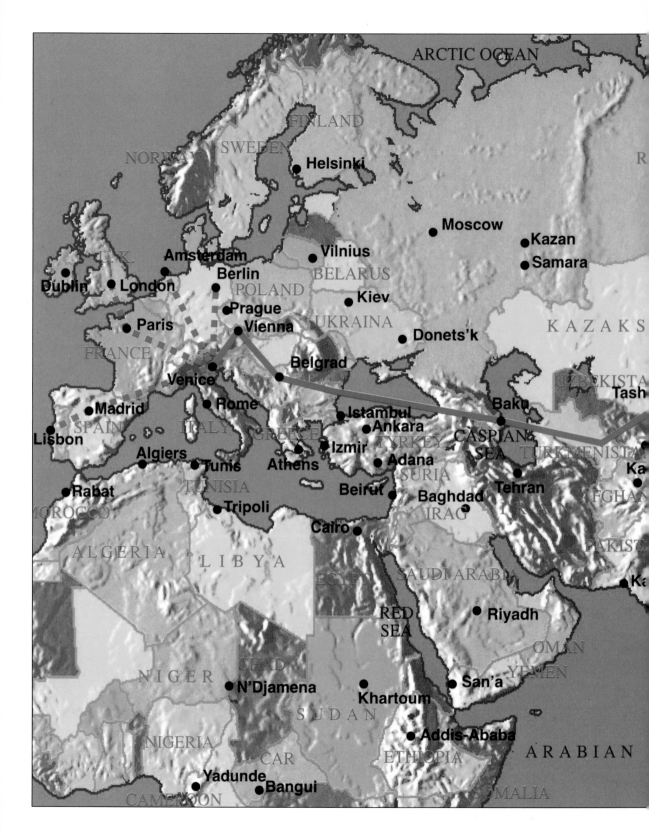

The Silk Road

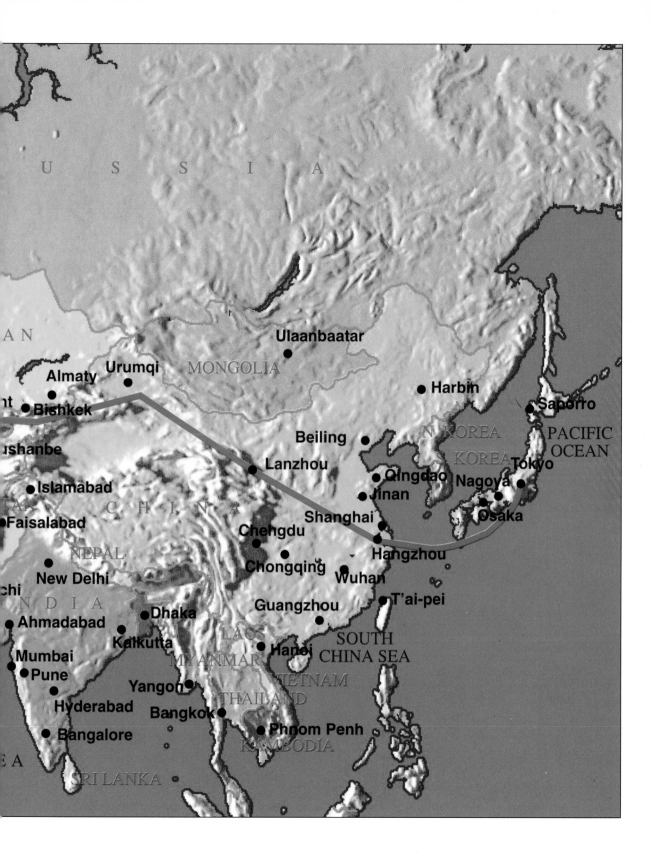

years, inflation is constantly decreasing and is now measured in single figures. According to forecasts of international experts growth rates of Azerbaijan's economy in 1997 were above five per cent and in 1998 about nine per cent.

According to the Government programme by the end of 2000, over seventy per cent of all state enterprises will be privatised and vouchers will become invalid. The Government is planning to open for privatisation such industries as electricity, communications, transport, energy and services. IBA (International Bank of Azerbaijan), the largest bank in the region, is being offered for sale.

Again, it is the important agricultural sector which exemplifies the pace and extent of reform, where as a result of radical land reform, the old system of *kolkhozes* and *sovkhozes* (collectives) has been broken up and currently ninety per cent of the country's agriculture is in private hands.

Private sector activities are mostly in new service industries (banking, insurance, computer, telecom), transport, construction and trade. Most of these activities, however, are concentrated around the capital city of Baku.

FOREIGN ECONOMIC POLICY

To ensure rapid, efficient reforms and overall development backed by rich natural resources, attraction of foreign capital is considered as one of the key factors of economic development. Favourable conditions are created and permanently improving for foreign investments. A legal framework provides good incentives for foreign investors. The completion, however, of building a legal and institutional market infrastructure is being gradually but consistently pursued. Thus, over 100 legal acts laying the ground for economic reforms have been passed by Parliament in recent years which include the Law on Protection of Foreign Investments, Property Law, Law on Agriculture, Land Code, Law on Privatisation of State Property, Law on Entrepreneurial Activity, Law on Securities and Stock Exchange, Anti-monopoly Law, Law on Bankruptcy and so on. Parliament approved the Land Law where over 60,000 families received property rights to land.

Major foreign investment is concentrated in the energy sector. Until now Azerbaijan managed to sign five major contracts for the development of its offshore oil resources amounting to about $20 bn. Cumulative investments into Azerbaijan during the next thirty years are expected to exceed $60 bn. The oil companies involved in these developments represent eleven countries (France, Iran, Italy, Japan, Norway, Russia, Saudi Arabia, Turkey, the UK and USA, including Azerbaijan) and others are also currently interested, such as Canada.

Apart from the oil and gas sector, however, foreign direct investments have not reached a significant figure.

FOREIGN DIRECT INVESTMENTS

Again, the increasing inflow of foreign direct investment (FDI) is concentrated in the oil and gas and related services and infrastructure. FDI committed by major players within the next three decades amounts to US$45-50 bn. The cumulative effect of these is modestly calculated at 1:3 ratio bringing the total volumes within the period up to US$150 bn. By the year 2000 FDI will constitute forty-five per cent of GDP.

above: Agricultural
production

opposite: Tea plantation

FDI by years (in millions US$):
1996 – 621, 1997 – 1223, 1998 – 1430

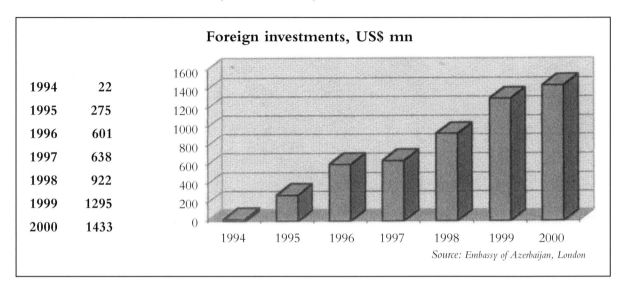

Foreign investments, US$ mn

1994	22
1995	275
1996	601
1997	638
1998	922
1999	1295
2000	1433

Source: Embassy of Azerbaijan, London

While in the first years the bulk of FDI concentrated on oil and oil related industries, in 1998 a third of FDI was directed to the non-oil sector. Major non-oil areas of interest to foreign investors are construction, services, manufacturing, transport and telecommunications.

The largest investors in Azerbaijan are the USA, the UK, Turkey, Germany and Japan.

Foreign trade volumes of Azerbaijan currently exceed $1.5 bn. At present, the country trades with more than sixty nations. The main trading partners, however, are Turkey, Russia, Iran, Ukraine, Germany and the UK.

Currently trade tariffs are unified at a level of average fifteen per cent, but liberalisation of the trade regime is progressing towards the requirements of World Trade Organisation accession.

Azerbaijan: Country Presentation   **Embassy of Azerbaijan, London**
Sources: ASSC, IMF

Selective Economic and Financial Indicators 1994–2000

	1994	1995	1996	1997	1998	1999	2000
Real GDP (%)	-21.2	- 11.0	1.2	5.1	7.6	8.4	10.6
Population (mn)	7.3	7.4	7.5	7.6	7.8	8.2	8.5
GDP per capita ($)		368	452	567	681	1,017	1,244
Inflation rate (%)	1,664	411.7	19.9	9.1	6.5	6.2	5.9
Exchange rate (m/US$)	1,457	4,416	4,305	3,947	3,749	3,562	3,384
Export, fob (m, US$)	682	680	849	962	1,397	1,802	2,497
Import fob (m, US$)	-845	-955	-1,318	-1,454	-2,157	-2,594	-2,660
Trade balance	-163	-275	-468	-492	-760	-792	-163
Current account balance	-121	-311	-654	-691	-991	-1,556	-1,344
Project loans (m,$)	54	14	19	86	151	176	192
Program loans (m, $)	0	102	31	0	0	0	0
Dir. & port. investm. (m, $)	22	275	601	638	922	1,433	1,295
Direct invest/GDP (%)	1.2	5.5	16.4	13.7	16.2	22	14.8
Overall balance (m, $)	-79	145	-39	-15	-18	18	119
Nominal GDP (m, $)	1,843	2,777	3,431	4,350	5,262	6,423	
Gross reserves (m, $)	2	119	245	387	463	527	589

INTERNATIONAL CO-OPERATION

Co-operation within the framework of international organisations constitutes one of the most significant guidelines of Azerbaijan's foreign economic policy. Azerbaijan is a member of more than twenty UN economic organisations including ESCAP (Economic and Social Commission for Asia and Pacific), UNIDO (United Nations Industrial Development Organisation), UNCTAD (United Nations Commission on Trade and Development), ECE (Economic Commission for Europe), IMO (International Maritime Organisation), WB (World Bank Group including International Development Association and International Financial Corporation), IMF (International Monetary Fund), observer status at the WTO (World Trade Organisation), as well as being a member of the EBRD (European Bank for Reconstruction and Development), IDB (Islamic Development Bank), partnership and co-operation with the European Union and the ADB (Asian Development Bank). There are agreements with other similar organisations who assist the country in transitional reforms and developing its economy.

Azerbaijan is also actively co-operating on the regional level as a member of such organisations as the CIS (Commonwealth of Independent States), BSEC (Black Sea Economic Co-operation), ECO (Economic Co-operation Organisation, which includes Turkey, Iran, Pakistan, Azerbaijan, the five Central Asian Republics and Afghanistan) and GUUAM (Georgia, Ukraine, Uzbekistan, Azerbaijan and Moldova).

opposite:
Memories of the
old 'Silk Road'

INTERNATIONAL PROJECTS

TRACECA (Transport Corridor for Europe, Caucasus and Asia): In September 1998 representatives of fourteen nations signed the Baku Declaration thus voting for the restoration of 'The Great Silk Road' (*see* map, pages 120-121). The project proposes to develop comprehensive transportation and communications infrastructure (rail, road, maritime, telecommunications) closely integrating all countries of the region.

There will be an associated Permanent Secretariat in Baku. This multi-billion-dollar project is supported by the EU and other major international organisations and all industrialised democracies. The US Senate endorsed a special act on 'The restoration of the Great Silk Road'.

Mountainous Garabagh

The conflict between Armenia and Azerbaijan over the Mountainous Garabagh region (Nagorno Karabakh in Russian; originally Daghlyg Garabagh in Azerbaijani), has been going on for more than ten years and derives from a misinterpretation of history and the territorial claims put forward by Armenia to Azerbaijan which run counter to international law.

History can never be the sole basis for discussions, but since Armenia has so often referred to it in relation to Mountainous Garabagh, Azerbaijan can demonstrate that the position of Armenia reflects a mistaken historical assumption.

The history of Garabagh – part of the Azerbaijan Republic which includes Daghlyg (mountainous) and Aran (lowland) Garabagh – is deeply rooted in antiquity and has always been an integral part of all state formations of Azerbaijan.

For a long period, the territory of Garabagh was part of a state in northern Azerbaijan – the kingdom of Caucasian Albania (as said earlier, not to be confused with the Albania of the Balkans) which began to emerge in the sixth to fourth centuries BC and ceased to exist in the eighth century AD. Later it was continuously part of other subsequent state formations ruled by dynasties of Azerbaijan, namely the Sajids (eighth to ninth centuries), the Salarids (tenth century), the Sheddadids (eleventh to twelfth centuries), the Atabey-Ildanizids (twelfth to thirteenth centuries), the Djalairids (thirteenth to fifteenth centuries), the Gara-Goyunlu (fifteenth century), the Sefevids (sixteenth to seventeenth centuries) and the

above: Refugee tent city,
Sabirabad

opposite: Refugee child in
Saatly camp

Refugee from
Zangelan

Qajars (eighteenth to nineteenth centuries).

It is worthwhile mentioning here, as an instance of the subordinate relationship between local rulers and their sovereigns, that in the fifteenth century Jahan-shah of the Gara-Goyunlu dynasty gave Hasan-Jalal, ruler of Garabagh, the title of 'melik'(from the Arabic for owner, lord, possessor or ruler).

The formation of the Azerbaijani nation experienced a struggle of different faiths and different political powers. At the time of the adoption of Christianity in Azerbaijan in the fourth century AD, Azerbaijan had a multi-ethnic and multi-confessional environment. Until the fourth century the population of Caucasian Albania, being ethnically Azerbaijani had professed a religion of fire-worship which consequently spread to Iran and developed into Zoroastrianism. Over the course of the historical development of Azerbaijan, Christianity and Islam prevailed at different times and, consequently, there were several splits within the Azerbaijani ethnos. When Caucasian Albania adopted Christianity as the state religion, some of the Azebaijanis who refused to become Christians continued to profess fire-worship. The chasm deepened when a considerable part of the population began to practise Islam. However, the autocephalic Albanian Church, founded in the sixth to seventh centuries AD, continued to exist until its abolition in 1836 by the Russian Tsarist government.

The Russian empire, acting in its own interests, used religion to gain influence in the region. To this end it abolished the independent Albanian Church and subordinated the Albanian Patriarchate to the Armenian Gregorian Church, which grew from 1441 onwards after the Azerbaijani Gara-Goyunlu dynasty decided to move the See of the Armenian Patriarchate from Cilicia to Echmiadzin, close to Iravan (the original Azerbaijani pronunciation

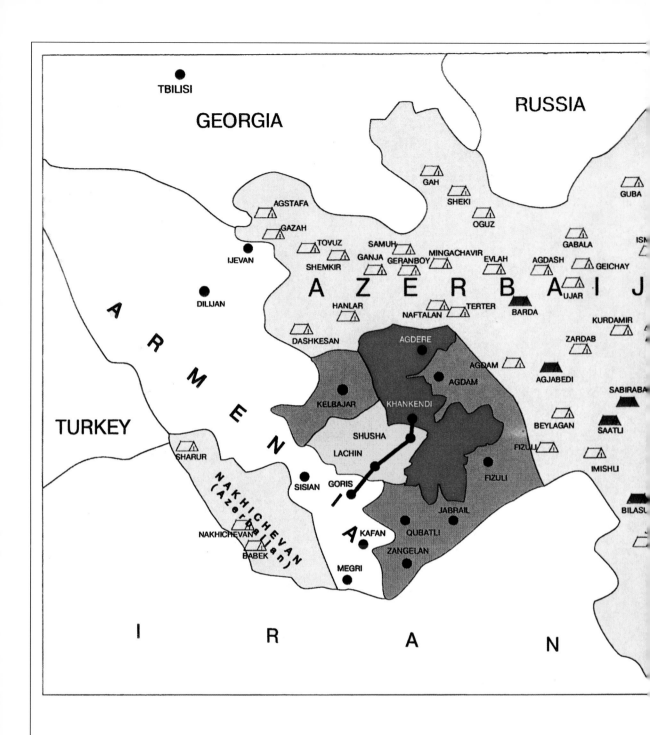

Territories of the Mountainous Garabagh region of the Azerbaijan Republic for which the Republic of Armenia demands the status of international legal party (4388 sq.km).

Azeri-populated territories which the Republic of Armenia could evacuate on condition that the Mountainous Garabagh region of the Azerbaijan Republic is given the status of international legal party.

Kelbajar region	– 1936 sq.km
Fizuli region	– 1386 sq.km
Qubatli region	– 802 sq.km
Jabrail region	– 1059 sq.km
Zangelan region	– 707 sq.km
Agdam region	– 1093 sq.km
total	– 6983 sq.km

Azeri-populated territories that the Republic of Armenia is not willing to evacuate under the pretext of creating a corridor between the Republic of Armenia and the Mountainous Garabagh region of the Azerbaijan Republic.

Lachin region   – 1835 sq.km
(Population – 59,500 Azerbaijanis)
Shusha region   – 970 sq.km
(Population – 29,500 Azerbaijanis)

total   – 2805 sq.km
Population – 89,000 Azerbaijanis)

Total area of the territories of the Azerbaijan Republic occupied by armed forces of the Republic of Armenia since the beginning of the conflict and which has undergone ethnic cleansing – 14,167 sq.km.
(Population – 837,000)

Refugee camps and places of settlement

Tent camp

of the capital of the independent Azerbaijani Irevan Khanate, conquered by the Russian empire– Yerevan in the present day). The Christian population of Albania was gradually forced into joining the Armenian Church.

Even when the local Caucasian Albanians of Garabagh embraced the Gregorian Armenian faith, some remained defiant and migrated to the left bank of the Kura River – their descendants still live in the village of Nij, north-west of Azerbaijan.

During 1909 and 1910 the Russian authorities connived with the Armenian Church to destroy local Albanian archives, including samples of Caucasian Albanian literature. Later, the Russian historian V L Velichko deplored these actions in both Caucasian Albania and Georgia, which had something of a similar experience.

Better to assess the appearance of the first ethnic Armenians in Azerbaijan in general and in Garabagh in particular, one would need also to look at the history of Armenia.

From the Middle Ages until the end of May 1918, Armenia was an assumed territory, only a concept, since there was no corresponding consistent administrative unit. The territory known today as the Republic of Armenia was shaped through international agreements in 1920 to 1921.

According to Armenian historians, the Armenian state was established in the sixth century BC in Asia Minor, albeit within the political control of Persian and then Roman overlords, until its demise in the fifth century AD. Then an Armenian kingdom was brought into existence in the ninth to fourteenth centuries AD. These developments all took place outside the Caucasus.

With the emergence of the Ottoman empire, which resulted in the loss of hope for a sovereign state, some Armenians moved northwards into the Caucasian heartland, which included such

Refugees in Saatly
camp

right: Refugee camp –
starting to build a
shelter

opposite: Refugees –
getting help

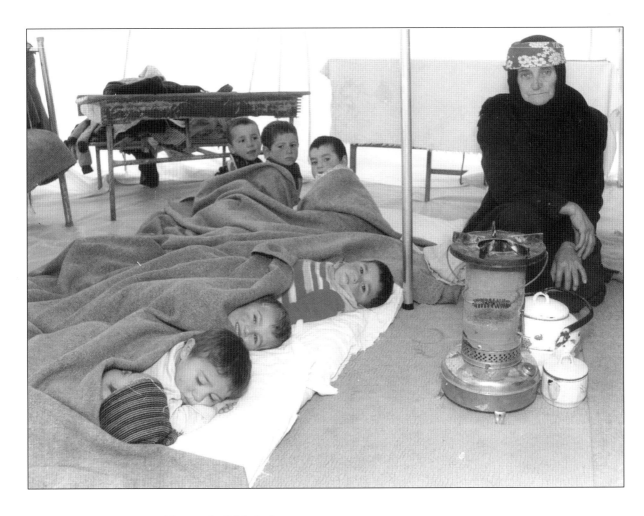

Nursery in Sabirabad
refugee camp

Azerbaijani strongholds as Ganja and Zengezur.

From the eighteenth century onwards the Armenians gained an ally – Russia – which used them in its rivalry with the Ottoman and Persian empires.

To ensure the success of its policy in the region, paying scant regard to the indigenous population's right to their own lands, Russia endeavoured to remove the indigenous inhabitants from their homes, particularly in the Azerbaijani provinces of Garabagh and Zengezur. By 1805 Russia was engaged in negotiations with the war-weary local rulers, particularly Ibrahim Khalil-Khan, the khan (governor) of the Azerbaijani independent Garabagh khanate (who named his fortress in Shusha 'Panahabad'), and also with the lords of the Sheki and Shemakha khanates. Through military conquest, Russia annexed the rest of the local Azerbaijani principalities of Lenkoran, Baky (Baku), Guba (Kuba), Ganja, Darband (Derbent) and, in 1826, the Azerbaijani khanates of Nakhchivan and Erevan.

Consequently, Russia had an interest in establishing a fellow Christian population of Armenians on the border of its empire, as a buffer against the local Azerbaijani khanates struggling to maintain their independence.

In 1828–1830 alone, in accordance with the Treaty of Turkmenchay, the Russian imperial government settled more than 130,000 Armenians from Iran and Turkey in the territories of the Azerbaijani khanates, including more than 50,000 in Garabagh. When Russia conquered the South Caucasus, the notion of 'Armenia' was not linked with a political, integral entity. Armenians were simply known as a Christian community among the Muslim majority within Azerbaijani states. Following the Treaty of Turkmenchay, however, Russia created a new administrative unit and called it the 'Armenian Oblast' (district), despite the Armenians constituting a minority. It included the Erevan, Nakhchivan and Ordubad districts of Azerbaijan. The Armenian Oblast was abolished in 1849 and replaced with the 'Erevan Gubernia', in accordance with the new structure of the administrative-territorial divisions within the Russian empire.

From the 19th century onwards the Armenians, despite their military and political weakness, tried to set a political agenda of their own (with the ultimate goal of creating an independent Armenian state) and to gain their utmost from the rivalry of the Great Powers in Anatolia and the South Caucasus. Between the Congress of Berlin and the San Stefano Conference in 1878 and the outbreak of the First World War in 1914, the emergence of the 'Armenian Question' gave rise to conflict.

Two Armenian ultra-nationalist parties were established ('Hunchak' in 1887 and 'Dashnaktsutyun' in 1890) which provided the ideological justification and organisational direction to the seizure of territories with steadily growing Armenian populations in the Caucasus. During that time, 500,000 Armenians were re-settled with Russian acquiescence from Iran and Turkey into the territory of Azerbaijan.

Russia took further steps favourable to the Armenians during the Balkan wars of 1912 to 1914 by proposing the creation of an autonomous 'Western Armenia' composed of the *vilayets* (districts) of Erzerum, Van, Bitlis, Diyarbakir, Harput and Sivas in Turkey. This proposal, however, was not supported by the European states, to the disappointment of the Hunchak and Dashnaktsutyun parties.

In typical imperial fashion, having settled Armenians into Azerbaijan, the Russian Tsarist government resorted to 'divide and rule' tactics by fomenting serious clashes between Armenians and

Young refugee

Azerbaijanis, particularly at a time when new liberation movements were growing in Azerbaijan and Georgia.

The ambitions of Armenian ultra-nationalists intent on creating their own state at the expense of Azerbaijan played into the hands of the Russian overlords, creating a coincidence of interests. These shared policies continued into the Soviet period.

The February and October Revolutions of 1917 in Russia marked a new stage in the 'Armenian Question'. In October 1917 the Armenian Congress convened in Tiflis (now Tbilisi, the capital of Georgia) and demanded the annexation by Russia of Eastern Turkey, occupied by the Russian Army during the First World War. On 31 December of the same year, the Council of People's Commissars adopted a decree, signed by Lenin and Stalin, on the right to self-determination of 'Turkish Armenia'.

On 28 May 1918, the first democratic state in the Muslim world, namely the Azerbaijan Democratic Republic, was established. One of the first steps taken by the government of the new country was to yield on the following day, 29 May 1918, the city of Iravan (as stated ealier, the capital of the former Azerbaijani Iravan khanate) to the Republic of Armenia, which had declared its independence one day prior to Azerbaijan, on 27 May 1918, but which as yet had no political centre. The territory of the Republic of Armenia at the time was limited to Iravan and Echmiadzin districts, both with fifty per cent Azerbaijani populations.

Nevertheless, the Armenian government, led by the Dashnak party (the 'Dashnaktsutyun'), claimed from Azerbaijan the territories of Nakhchivan, Zengezur and Garabagh, and this led to the war between Azerbaijan and Armenia of 1918-1920. Thousands of Azerbaijanis were killed on the battlefront as well as during the massacres committed by Dashnak-led Armenians in nearly all the

Imishli refugee camp

above: Refugee camp

opposite: Wounded
and traumatised from
the Ter Ter region

main towns of Azerbaijan. This conflict seriously undermined the struggle of Azerbaijan and the other states of the region to maintain their independence and sovereignty.

Little was done to stop the fighting while the Armenians attempted to seize more territory. For example, President Wilson of the United States accepted instructions from the League of Nations stating that Armenia 'cannot exist without support' and that its borders must be defined. However, the Senate decided that the 'Armenian Question' was a European issue and rejected the 'mandate on Armenia'. The French Government acted towards

Armenians in a similar way in connection with Cilicia, which had been occupied by France in 1919. France concluded a peace treaty with Turkey in 1921 and surrendered Cilicia. The 'Armenian Question' was, therefore, increasingly focussed on the South Caucasus and bitter fighting took place in the contested regions. It did not cease with the invasion by the 11th Red Army and the annihilation by the Bolsheviks of Azerbaijan's independence and the establishment of Soviet power on 28 April 1920.

The Dashnak Armenian government continued to wage war in the same areas of Garabagh, Nakhchivan and Zengezur until November 1920, when the entire Dashnak government was overthrown by Soviet Russia. This did not, however, lead to a solution of the territorial dispute.

A joint letter was written in 1920 by Nariman Narimanov, the Chairman of the Revolutionary Committee of Azerbaijan; B Mdivani, an ethnic Georgian member of the Caucasus Regional Committee (the Bolshevik Kav Bureau, responsible for all of the Caucasus); A Mikoyan, an ethnic Armenian and member of the Central Committee of the Communist Party of Azerbaijan; and even A Nourijanian, an Armenian and member of the Central Committee of the Communist Party of Armenia. The letter, addressed to the People's Commissar for Foreign Affairs, G Chicherin, and to S Orjonikidze, also of the Committee for the Caucasus, declared that: 'As far as the supposedly disputed territories of Zengezur and Garabagh, that have already joined Soviet Azerbaijan, are concerned, we categorically state that there can be no dispute about these places and they must stay within Azerbaijan . . . The regions of Julfa and Nakhchivan are populated solely by Muslims . . . and must join Azerbaijan'.

S Orjonikidze went even further in his telegrams to Lenin, Stalin

Refugees, a young
family

Azerbaijan

above: Refugees resting

opposite: A refugee
from Aghdam, on the
Aghdam–Barda road

and Chicherin, stressing the traditional economic attachment of Garabagh and Zengezur to Baku and Azerbaijan. Mikoyan also declared that 'agents of the non-Soviet Armenian government, the Dashnaks, are striving for annexation of Garabagh by Armenia, but for the population of Garabagh this would mean being deprived of their lifeline, Baku, so as to be connected to Erevan with which it has not ever been linked in any way'.

The Armenian Soviet Socialist Republic, however, continued to press the same territorial claims as its predecessors. Responding to these demands, the Caucasus Bureau of the Central Committee of the Russian Communist Party decided at its meeting of 5 July 1921 that: 'Proceeding from the necessity to maintain ethnic peace between Muslims and Armenians, economic ties between Mountainous and Lowland Garabagh and its uninterrupted ties with Azerbaijan, Mountainous Garabagh is to be retained within the Azerbaijan Soviet Socialist Republic and to be granted broad regional autonomy with an administrative centre in Shusha, which is a part of the autonomous region.' In 1922, the Azerbaijan Soviet Socialist Republic was absorbed by the USSR.

By the decision of 7 July 1923, the Soviet Azerbaijan Central Executive Committee created for Mountainous Garabagh the status of Autonomous Region – the 'Nagorno Karabakh Autonomous Oblast' (NKAO) – a legal entity within the Azerbaijan SSR. The administrative centre of the NKAO was moved from Shusha to Khankendi (whose name was changed to 'Stepanakert' later in the same year by Armenians to honour Stepan Shaumian, a prominent Armenian Bolshevik). The boundaries of 'Nagorno Karabakh' were drawn artificially so as to ensure an Armenian majority in this ethnically mixed region – even though it had only been achieved around 1840. Official Tsarist population records indicate that the population of Garabagh, like other areas of the Caucasus, was overwhelmingly 'Muslim' prior to the mass migrations of Armenians (numbering more than 50,000) from Iran as provided for in the treaty of Turkmenchay which ended the Russo-Persian War of 1826-1828. This majority was used as the basis for the artificial creation of an Armenian entity.

The policy of the Soviet Union was far from even-handed. Several points have to be made here. For example, in contrast with the 'NKAO' and its 138,600 Armenian and 47,500 Azerbaijani population (1989), neither the central government of the USSR nor the Armenian SSR had ever considered the possibility of granting even some status of cultural autonomy to the 300,000 Azerbaijanis residing compactly in Armenia (given the fact that Azerbaijan's population at the time was 7 million in comparison to Armenia's population of 3 million). Moreover, many of them were forcibly deported from Armenia, particularly in 1948-1950. Ethnic cleansing of all Azerbaijanis from Armenia was finalised in 1988-1989.

It also has to be mentioned here that the Bolsheviks did not return to Azerbaijan the territories lost in previous battles: in 1921 the Soviet government legalised Armenia's hold on Zengezur, thus driving a wedge between the Azerbaijan SSR mainland and its province of Nakhchivan. From then on, Nakhchivan was isolated. The following year, in 1922, Dilijan and Geycha were also transferred from Azerbaijan to the Armenian SSR. A number of villages were also transferred to Armenia without reciprocity from Nakhchivan in 1929, from Gedebey in 1969 and, as late as 1984, from the Gazakh district.

During the Soviet period, as a result of land transfers from Azerbaijan to Armenia, the territory of Azerbaijan shrank from

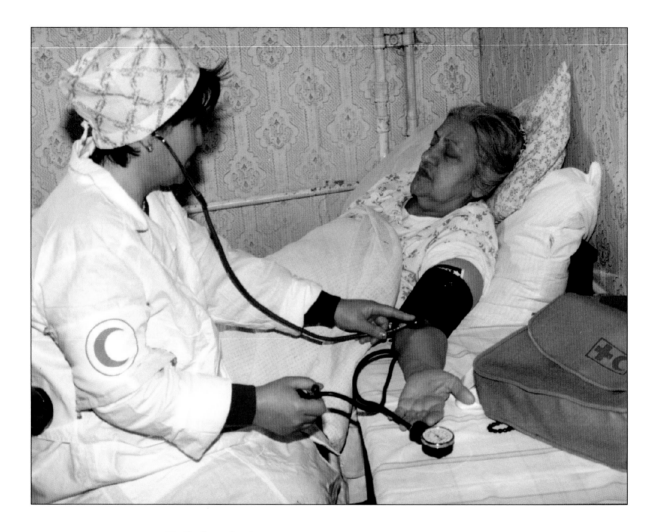

**Medical service in a
refugee camp**

113,900 sq. km in 1920 (while still independent) to 86,600 sq. km in 1988 under the Soviet Union.

Armenian expansionist ambitions, so skilfully exploited by the central authorities in Moscow to create havoc in the regions, eventually led in the late 1980s to the terrible aggression and calamity which has blighted the whole area for more than a decade. One in seven Azerbaijanis is now a refugee or a displaced person, driven from Mountainous Garabagh or from their homes elsewhere in surrounding areas or from Armenia.

Neither history nor oppression can justify the Armenian territorial claims which led to the conflict. The government of Azerbaijan is, therefore, committed to seeking a peaceful solution to the tragic conflict and to the elimination of all its consequences including, first of all, evacuation of all the occupied territories and the return of the Azerbaijani population to their homes.

Nakhchivan

The history and politics of the Nakhchivan Autonomous Republic have not been that different to those of Nagorno Garabagh, except that in the recent conflict it has not been at the centre of the fighting in the same way.

Nakhchivan occupies the south-western end of the Dereleyez and Zengezur chain of mountains of the Lesser Caucasian Range. It is wedged between Armenia, (which cuts it off entirely from the Azerbaijan mainland to which it belongs), and a continuous border with Iran and a few kilometres with Turkey on its south-west frontier. Most traffic is airborne, which is very limiting. For any goods or passengers to reach Nakhchivan overland from the rest of Azerbaijan, they have to travel along an uncertain route inside Iran and enter the territory from there. Without the free flow of transport through Armenia the autonomous republic is in a virtual blockade and so they, more than anyone, are desirous of a peaceful resolution to the dispute with Armenia so that the embargo against them can be lifted. The region has a rich history and lucrative natural resources but tourism and economic development are almost impossible in these isolated conditions, particularly being deprived of virtually all sources of energy.

Nakhchivan is rich in natural resources. There are rock salt, rare metals, arsenic, gypsum, marble, dolomites and mineral waters used in medical treatment. Its flora and fauna are also remarkable and some of its landscapes are exceptionally beautiful. There are also interesting monuments which testify to the long history of human habitation since the beginning of time. The early fortresses of Oghlangala and Govurgala in Sherur district were built to protect the region from invaders. It was taken over by the Sasanid rulers in medieval times. Byzantine, Persian, Arab, Georgian, Turkish and other sources describe its history and character. The city of Nakhchivan is mentioned admiringly.

It was an important transit route and part of the Silk Road. There were at least 150,000 inhabitants at the time and local art and trade developed in parallel. Politically it had a lively history too. The Hurrami movement in the early ninth century when Azerbaijanis resisted Arab rulers had a significant presence in Nakhchivan. Earlier, however, the inhabitants were considered loyal enough for the Sasanids to mint their money in Nakhchivan which was used throughout their empire.

Towards the end of the tenth century and following the feudal states of Sajiler and Salariler, as they were called locally, the Nakhchivan Shahlyghy was created which only succumbed in 1064 to the Seljuk Turks. Its importance continued to grow until 1175 when the capital of the local Atabeyler-Eldenizler state was transferred to Tabriz further south.

It never regained its former prominence despite its historical role. The Mongol invasions, those of the Golden Horde, the fighting between the Sefevid and Ottoman military orders on its territory and later the invasions of Shah Abbas I all eroded the local autonomy which Nakhchivan had once enjoyed. Shah Abbas actually resettled some of the local population in Mazandaran, Isfahan, Kahsana and other places. Furthermore, some of the neighbouring feudal lords, of Kartli-Kakheti and the khans of Garabagh and Erevan also made attempts to incorporate Nakhchivan into their orbit.

Mountain shepherds

There are nevertheless still traces of Nakhchivan's former glory among the ruins and monuments. The architect Abu Bakr Ajemi who lived in the twelfth century helped develop two styles of architecture which strongly influenced that of the rest of the Near and Middle East which are seen in the Momine-Khatun and Yusif Ibn Guseyr mausoleums. There was also the famous Elinje fortress which resisted Tamerlane's siege of fourteen years' duration.

As a result of the Russo-Persian wars in the early nineteenth century, Nakhchivan was also occupied by Russia, together with other territories of Azerbaijan, and according to the Treaty of Turkmenchay in 1828 was annexed to Russia together with the Erevan khanate. One of the conditions of the treaty worthy of attention was, as mentioned earlier, that there was a provision for the relocation of Armenians, who had been living in the territories of Iran and Turkey, into the territory of Azerbaijan, including the Nakhchivan and Erevan khanates. The ethnic balance, however, did not change significantly until the establishment of the Soviet Union in the region. Nevertheless, despite the Azeri majority, imperial Russian government policy skilfully used the mixed population to create unrest in order to quell the demands for political independence.

During the nineteenth century, however, a number of secular schools were opened in Nakhchivan and a prominent intelligentsia emerged which made a significant contribution to Azerbaijan culture. There was the famous teacher Mammad Taghy Sidgi, and the writer who is considered to be a forerunner of Azerbaijani realism, Mirza Jalil Mamedguluzade, the poet-dramatist Huseyn Javid and a whole line of novelists such as Mammad Said Ordubadi, Aligulu Gemkusar, Eynali Sultanov, Aziz Sharifov and Mammadagha Shakhtakhtinski, all associated with Nakhchivan.

When the Tsarist government fell, fighting broke out when the Armenians, led by Andronik, attempted to take Nakhchivan. In November 1918, a state structure called the 'Araz-Turkish Republic' was established here and it lasted until March 1919. It included the following regions: Sharur, Dereleyez, Ordubad, Serdarabad, Ulukhanly, Gemerli and Mehri. The capital of the republic was Nakhchivan.

After the First World War Nakhchivan had been included in the area of influence of the United Kingdom. British armed forces had been brought here in January 1919 and they declared Nakhchivan a non-aligned zone and created their general-governorship here. When the British recognised the independence of the Azerbaijan Democratic Republic, the new Azerbaijan government established a Nakhchivan general-governorship and appointed Bahram-khan Nakhchivanski as a governor-general. The Armenian side tried to establish a similar 'Armenian administration' but were unsuccessful, even when they attempted, after the British left Nakhchivan in late 1919 and were replaced by the USA, to establish a pro-Armenian American general-governorship.

On 23 November 1919 with the mediation of the USA an agreement was signed between Azerbaijan and Armenia in Tiflis, the capital of Georgia. The Armenians were encouraged not to respect its provisions by the Russians who sent them illicit assistance. It in turn facilitated the invasion by the 11th Russian Army which overthrew the independence of Azerbaijan in 1920. By July 1920 Nakhchivan was also occupied by the Bolshevik invading army and on 28 July the Nakhchivan Soviet Socialist Republic was proclaimed. It was declared an inseparable part of the Azerbaijan SSR. As in Garabagh, the Armenians did not relinquish their claims to Nakhchivan either, even after Soviet power had been established in Armenia. As a result of the 1921 referendum on whether or not Nakhchivan should be a part of Azerbaijan, ninety per cent of the population voted for being left as they were, within Azerbaijan. This was further confirmed in the Moscow Treaty signed by Russia and Turkey on 16 March 1921 and in the Kars Treaty signed by Russia, Azerbaijan, Georgia, Armenia and Turkey in October 1921.

In February 1923 the local Nakhchivan Soviet Congress proclaimed the establishment of the Nakhchivan Autonomous Region and later, in early 1924, an Autonomous Republic within the Azerbaijan SSSR.

The next phase of Nakhchivan's history was typically Soviet: the late 1920s and early 1930s saw the establishment of several industrial enterprises and during the Second World War a strong contribution to the war effort. An important war hero from Nakhchivan was Major-General Akim Abbasov who distinguished himself in combat. Others were Gezenfer Akberov, Nejefgulu Rafiyev and Abbas Guliyev who were all given awards as Heroes of the Soviet Union, as well as Colonel Mehdi Mahmudov.

After the war more industrial enterprises were built and agrarian activity was transformed into a thriving agrarian-industrial sphere. In the late 1980s, however, an economic recession began there as it did in mainland Azerbaijan and the rest of the USSR.

Under 'Perestroyka' in the same period, the political situation in the USSR changed. Forces struggling for national interests created a structure called the Azerbaijani Popular Front (APF). Nakhchivan's section of the APF became even more active. It took an unprecedented step with the initiative on 31 December 1989 to destroy the Soviet border post in order to cross over and embrace for the first time relatives they had not been able to see on the other side. This concerned the border with Iran but attempts on 7 January 1990 were made to reach Turkey as well. By 19 January of the same year, the governing body of the time, the Supreme Soviet of the Autonomous Republic of Nakhchivan, voted to withdraw from the USSR. This was one of the reasons which prompted the Soviet government to order the army into Baku where they committed, as already mentioned, the atrocities referred to ever since as 'Black January'. By the summer of 1990, Heydar Aliev, later to play an important role as President of the whole country, returned to his native Nakhchivan and became chairman of the local parliament. Nakhchivan took even further defiant action, removing by act of local parliament on 17 November 1990 the words 'Soviet Socialist' from their emblem and flying the formerly independent national Azerbaijan flag, but by the end of 1990 the Soviet Union ceased to exist and independence became a reality, with Nakhchivan an integral part of the new Azerbaijan Republic.

On 28 May 1991, the 'Hope' Sederek-Diluju bridge between Nakhchivan and Turkey was opened. Finally, in the first Constitution of the independent Azerbaijan Republic, adopted on 12 November 1995, it was made an Autonomous State and on 28 April 1998 it obtained its own constitution.

Nakhchivan also hopes for a peaceful solution to the dispute with Armenia. This will lead to the end of the blockade it suffers, so that it can offer its hospitality and the development of its resources without impediment.

Musicians in the old caravanserai, Baku

List of illustrations

Index